NetEASY Marketing

WES MELCHER

INFINITY
PUBLISHING

Copyright © 2012 by Wes Melcher

ISBN 978-0-7414-7968-6 Paperback
ISBN 978-0-7414-7969-3 Hardcover
ISBN 978-0-7414-7970-9 eBook
Library of Congress Control Number: 2012916456

Printed in the United States of America

Published September 2012

INFINITY PUBLISHING
1094 New DeHaven Street, Suite 100
West Conshohocken, PA 19428-2713
Toll-free (877) BUY BOOK
Local Phone (610) 941-9999
Fax (610) 941-9959
Info@buybooksontheweb.com
www.buybooksontheweb.com

Acknowledgements

This book has been one of the most challenging projects I have ever completed and I would not have the ability to share this information with you if my amazing parents had not believed in me and encouraged me throughout my entire life. To Sara, who has partnered with me in raising our incredible daughter, thank you for allowing me to chase my dreams around the world. To my precious daughter Jianna, you are my sunshine and everything I do is for you.

To my Brother and Sister, thank you for putting up with me. To my incredible mentors: Mike Azcue, Wayne Nugent, Marc Accetta, Eddie Head, John Carpenter, and Jeff Nixon, thank you for helping to mold my views on business and teach me the concepts that have allowed me to impact hundreds of thousands of people around the globe. Thank you to my editors, this book would not have been possible without your guidance and support. Lastly, to my Teams around the world, thank you for believing in me and allowing me to be part of your journey.

Table of Contents

1

Network Marketing 2.0

*M*y career in the Direct Sales Industry has spanned more than 15 years. I have always been an entrepreneur, starting multiple companies before even graduating high school. While most kids were thinking about how to start a lemonade stand or earn cash by mowing lawns, I was thinking about hiring other kids my age to do that kind of work for me so I could multiply my earnings. So in some sense, I have been building teams and recruiting for as long as I can remember. My entire family has the ability to do what we want, when we want, how we want, and the way we want every day because of this industry and because of what I am about to share with you in this book. We don't own alarm clocks, we've taken more than 100 vacations over the last seven years, we have given graciously to our favorite charities and we have changed the lives of thousands around us, helping several people become millionaires. I wake up when I want to, go to sleep when I want to, take vacations when and where I want to, spend time with my family, and best of all, there is no such thing as a long weekend or "holiday weekend," because every day is a holiday if I want it to be. I don't have to keep waiting for the weekend to come because I am able to do what I want, when I want.

These are the perks of the business for people trying to re-shape their lives by having success in this industry. Most people in the traditional workplace daydream about when the work day will be over, or when they will have the courage to leave their current job, or how long it will be before they can do what they really want to do instead of what they *have* to do. If you are among the overwhelming majority of people who would not be in the job they currently have if they didn't have bills to pay, **this book will answer a lot of your questions about network marketing, and may very well be your ticket to freedom and fulfillment**. If, however, you are one of the lucky ones who love your job, then use this book to help you make more money so that you can continue to do the job you love for *free*. If you're already pursuing the dream of financial freedom and total independence through the direct sales or network marketing industry, and you are looking for an edge on the competition, then congratulations on choosing this book and taking the time to develop your skills.

I am grateful to be on this journey with you. We're going to have a lot of fun in this book, and I am going to give you most of the knowledge that I have gained living my dream over the last 15 years. You do know that the "dream" of doing what you want, how you want, on your own terms and in your own way, is not just a dream, don't you? This dream is very real, believe me; it is worth every hour you work, every sacrifice you make, and every ounce of dedication you can muster up to get to the realization that you can manifest your dreams.

You can manifest your dreams!

Total lifestyle freedom is one of the shining achievements of this industry today, and thanks to technology and the Internet, people are experiencing higher levels of success than ever before. Today, direct sales and network marketing have hit the mainstream. Former presidents are applauding the industry, and nationally televised media hosts have raved about why direct sales companies are the "best performing companies" during a recession. Robert Kiyosaki and Donald Trump have both written books on why they feel Direct Sales and Network Marketing are the best ways for someone with a small amount of capital and very little experience to create *generational wealth*. This wealth is not just for you now, but for your children and grandchildren as well. In fact, there isn't a week that goes by where someone doesn't approach me with a new concept or product being sold via direct sales or network marketing.

Be grateful you're reading this book in the 21st and not the 20th century. Network marketing has changed dramatically over the last couple of decades, and so has the way home-based businesses are perceived, and by extension, the freedom to work from home. The assumption 15 to 20 years ago was that if you worked a home-based business, you either didn't have a job or couldn't get one. Network marketing was viewed as the only way for some people who had little or no options in traditional business to try to earn a living. Those who embraced network marketing in the past were not only limited by the negative perception of the industry, but also by the shortcomings of technology. Those early pioneers looked forward to a day when technology would complement their business and when the negative perception around the industry would shift. Well, that day has come. Just take a look at what Paul Zane Pilzer, an award-winning economist who has worked with numerous U.S. presidents has to say in his book "The Next Millionaires":

> Today, the U.S. and the world economy look almost identical to how they looked in 1991, except that there are more opportunities for entrepreneurs due to recent changes in taxation and technology. Based on this history and current conditions, I forecast that U.S. household wealth will again double to $100 trillion by 2016—and that over the same ten years, the exploding U.S. economy will create at least ten million new millionaires. For those of you in the direct selling industry, this is incredibly good news. Why? Because a significant, good number of those new ten million millionaires are the people who are entering your businesses at this very moment.[1]

In this book, I will show you the *new age* of network marketing. These are not your mother's and father's network marketing strategies. With the creation of social networks and web 2.0, coupled with the increasing social desire to be part of someone's network club or organization, technology and society have made it easier than ever to stay in touch and network, and I am going to show you how to take advantage of these changes and turn a half-century-old industry into a stream of wealth and influence. I will walk you through how to leverage revolutionary concepts that have allowed me to build teams and networks in the hundreds of thousands.

For many industries and companies, the term "2.0" is synonymous with evolution and new generations of development. When you see "2.0" after software titles, for instance, it conveys an improvement on the first edition. "2.0" has even been used to describe the new landscape of the Internet consisting of the influx of social media and the birth of new consumer-driven websites and applications for phones and mobile devices. Several industries and technologies have gone through this type of rebirth and revitalization, but none so much as network marketing. The network marketing industry today is nothing like it was 50 years ago, or even 10 years ago. This is the New Age of network marketing and this book is designed to help you understand how to take advantage of these changes.

The virtual landscape provided by technology even a decade ago was not what it is today. Today, we enjoy the benefits of a sophisticated, ever-expanding culture of technology that spans the world. Unforeseen by even the most tenured analysts and executives, even Fortune 500 companies are getting in on the action, becoming part of the global network of communication and connectivity, offering top-level employees the flexibility to work from home. This is truly the age of the "Netrepreneur," and more and more people than ever before, from business moguls to housewives, are using the Internet to make money hand over fist, running successful businesses out of the comfort of their own homes.

Today *everyone* wants the freedom and flexibility to work from home. And due to this paradigm shift, the perception of network marketing, once questioned as viable or credible, has become a sign of sustainability and real innovation. Because of this new awareness, more people are receptive to the idea of this enterprise, and the desire to work from home has helped boost the credibility and enhance the benefits of the direct sales, multi-level marketing (MLM) and network marketing industries dramatically. Since most network marketing companies promote an enhanced lifestyle, personal freedom, business ownership and being in control of your own life, these factors have become a selling point for every company no matter what products or services they offer.

In the current social media landscape, large companies have figured out what people in the direct sales industry have known for years—"word-of-mouth advertising is the most *powerful* form of advertising available." We are living in an age of social networking, and "social proof" is what every company is looking for in today's economy. Companies want to be "Liked" so people will recommend their products and services to their entire "network." Today companies are realizing what consumers say about them on Twitter, YouTube, Facebook, Pinterest and other social media outlets really does matter. Fortune 500 companies are building entire divisions of people to dissect, promote and understand how to leverage social media and consumer channels to improve their brand and increase awareness of their products.

Direct sales companies have known for decades that the fastest, cheapest and easiest way to get a product to market is via direct sales. Now, because of the massive growth of companies like Facebook, traditional corporations are coming to the realization that a YouTube video made by a 10 year-old may be more powerful than the $3 million they spent on a Super Bowl ad.

Such a realization has led to a surprising turn of events. Companies are actually hiring individuals with large YouTube followings to create custom videos to help with product launches and to attract fans. And, have you noticed, more and more corporations are producing commercials that ask viewers to check them out on social sites for more information about their product at the end of the commercial? Think about that for a moment. Today's mega corporations are so enamored with social media that they are asking people to visit them on these sites in the middle of their traditional advertising! What's more, they're rewarding their fans and loyal followers with discounts, coupons and special information if they check out their page on social sites. The lure of the social network, and word-of-mouth advertising has never been as strong as it is right now. The days of traditional advertising are numbered. Sure, there will always be magazines, billboards, commercials and newspapers, but the role they once played has narrowed, and their clout will never be the same in the world of consumer marketing.

This is where we come in. The opportunity to make money in direct sales and network marketing is greater than ever. Not only is there more information and technology at your fingertips to help you succeed, but there are more companies, more products and more ideas coming out of this industry than ever before. Twenty years ago the only way you could hear about a network marketing company was in person or over the phone. Today, the mediums for spreading information and ideas to people are greater than they have ever been in history.

Not only is technology a benefit for representatives and distributors, but the companies in this industry have the ability to calculate more complex compensation, pay faster, communicate more effectively, disseminate and bundle information, and grow their businesses quicker than ever before—which means there is ample opportunity for everyone to benefit. Today, technology makes it easier to connect with customers, build teams and grow networks, which makes it easier to expand and maintain your business.

Just for a moment, imagine having to use a "phone tree" to get in touch with your team. For those of you who don't know what this is, it was basically a system of making a call to several people who, in turn, were responsible for making calls to a designated group of people, who were then responsible for making calls to even more people. Today, we can communicate to a vast group in an instant and basically accomplish the same thing with very little human error. What's more, we can even designate groups for communication purposes according to their location, demographics or relationship. This speeds the method of delivery and allows you to focus on individuals, while eliminating miscommunication. It's also just a simple example of how technology has improved our lives as representatives and distributors.

Just think about what it was like for companies to try to calculate commissions for thousands of representatives on a weekly or monthly basis without computers or software! The complexity and intricacies of back office software and accounting technology have also had a hand in changing network marketing, improving communication and allowing companies to have less people on staff physically tabulating commissions or providing oversight on basic accounting processes. This has dramatically lowered overhead for companies in our industry, requiring less capital for startup, and resulting in more ideas making it to the marketplace. The advancement of technology for MLM and network marketing companies has also allowed for the development of new compensation plans and creative pay structures, all of which would have been virtually impossible to pay or even track 20 years ago. This is actually one of the places where the origin of the term multi-level marketing developed. In the past, companies were limited to the levels they could pay based purely on them being able to calculate the compensation. Of course, today technology is so advanced that there are countless ways companies can choose to pay commissions, bonuses or overrides due to the evolution of computers and accounting software.

The perception of network marketing, once questioned as viable or credible, has become a sign of sustainability and real innovation.

The advancements in technology and the expansion of social media have given the *entire* direct sales and network marketing industries a brand new life. The benefit of this positive perception means that representatives no longer have to hide their profession or be afraid to talk about their business opportunity or products. The days of disguising what you are selling to try to trick someone into listening or joining, are over. In fact, when I train new representatives, I find myself reminding them that there is no reason to deceive their potential prospects or customers. Running your business with **integrity will produce results** that are more duplicable because people will feel like what you are doing is honest and ethical. If representatives have an internal conflict with what they are selling, it will make them incongruent, and they will feel like they have to dupe people into signing up. There are many strategies and ways to coach team members on how to expose the business or products properly. Due to this newfound acceptance of the industry, people feel comfortable inviting friends to a dinner party or event to hear about their business or products.

The ways to expose potential customers and prospects to your company are increasing. I will go through several of them with you throughout this book so you can use them effectively, and with confidence. Parties and events can be used to build or promote any type of business no matter what the product or service you are selling—even if you think your product cannot be promoted with the "party method." We will delve into these methods and technologies later in the book, but once again this just reiterates that the old school days of network marketing are over. If you are still reading books or listening to CDs that talk about bait and switch, or hiding what you are trying to sell, then you will probably wind up with disgruntled friends and family. If, however, you use the methods I talk about here, not only will you have success with your business, you will also grow your social network to astronomical levels.

Of course, exposing ideas and presenting to prospects is just one aspect of this industry. There are several books out there that offer to teach you how to become the "ultimate presenter" or the "bulldog closer." This book, however, will take an in-depth look at *today's* methods and strategies that have allowed me to build a global business comprising thousands of customers and distributors worldwide. I have used many of these strategies for more than half of my life to train hundreds of thousands of people and create multi-million-dollar-producing teams with a variety of products, and employing completely different approaches to marketing, selling and recruiting. I have been able to draw from my experience in sales, training, management, marketing, social media and promotion to create a book which has not been available until now. I have made it my life's mission to improve myself, my methods, my approach and my skills as I have evolved throughout my career. The following chapters will illustrate and expand on my methodologies, all from a down-to-earth, easy-to-understand point of view. It is my sincere hope that you implement these tools into your business, no matter what product or service you promote, so you can, once and for all, live the life you have always dreamed of.

It is time to turn NetWORK Marketing into NetEASY Marketing!

---

[1] Pilzer, P. Z. (2006). *The Next Millionaires*. Retrieved from www.paulzanepilzer.com.

2

Starting from Scratch

*I*f you grew up in the 80s or were born before 1984, you've probably heard of "Six Degrees of Kevin Bacon." The gist of the game is that you can connect any actor or actress to the actor Kevin Bacon by the movies they have appeared in with less than six connections. In other words if you take any actor or actress you can connect them with someone that they have acted with, who has acted with someone, who has acted with someone, who has acted with someone, who has acted with Kevin Bacon. If you haven't heard of it, you're probably familiar with the concept of "Six Degrees of Separation." Likewise, the idea behind it is that we can connect to just about anyone on the planet through six people we know. Think about that for a moment, because it's an incredible idea illustrating how life itself is a network, and from most studies I have heard about, the phenomena of connectivity isn't "six degrees" as most people think, but actually much less today due to the growth of technology and online communication.

The real beauty of connectivity becomes clear when looking at how fast teams can grow in the direct sales or network marketing industries. In today's sea of social media and technology, we are able to efficiently cast a wide net, connecting globally with only a few intermediaries. Now, here is my proposal: if you're networking properly and recruiting the right types of people, you can make a connection with just about anyone in the world through "Two Degrees of Separation." That means you should be able to find the people you want to bring into your business, or better yet, the specific person you want to bring into your business, with just two intermediaries. This also means you can literally build an entire team of customers and distributors with just one or two key people.

No matter which company you work with or what products you sell, in network marketing you have to account for your initial list. It is the lifeline of your business and is a viable pathway to build success from the ground up. But where do you begin? Put another way, who, among your friends, family and associates should get the opportunity to hear about what you are doing before anyone else?

The Hit List

Your list should never stop growing. I call my prospective customer or distributor list my "hit list" and I am constantly adding and subtracting people from it. Even to this day, after being in the direct sales industry since 1997, I still actively seek out, prospect and bring on new customers and recruits. New customers are the lifeblood of any direct sales business. *The size of your business begins with your hit list and that list begins with you.*

The Warm Market Approach

When it comes to planning the makeup of your initial list, consider taking the warm market approach. This method has proved invaluable to my efforts in this industry, and I have seen brand new direct sales representatives consistently use this approach to their advantage. Actually, the warm market approach has made me millions, and in this chapter, I'll share the basics of this method so you can do so as well. Even with a diversity of products and services, the tenets of this approach remain the same.

In the instance of making your initial list, it's OK to start with the path of least resistance. Build up momentum from your own contacts, establishing connections that are the easiest to make and maintain. Start your list of potential customers or prospects with your warm market first. If that seems uncomfortable or awkward, please understand this—it's much easier to get someone to listen to you if they know you, like you or trust you. Some people are masters of building rapport, while others struggle to get their ideas across, and establish real connections with people. Building rapport with customers or prospects is easier if you already have a relationship with them. This is referred to as the warm market. When you draw from people you know, it results in one less hurdle to overcome, and it automatically gives you an advantage because they already like you and trust you. If you don't have a relationship with a prospect, you have to gain their trust first; however, if you're already familiar with the prospect, then you can move on to the next step.

This will let you hit the ground running. Get a sheet of paper out right now (take a moment right now and *do it!*) and start making a list of potential prospects and customers. Even if you've gone through this list process before, do it again; there may be people you have left off or forgotten. The good news is that we're living in the information age and thanks to social networking sites, you can find just about anyone you've met in your life on the Internet. Please take the time to do this exercise before we proceed. After you build your list, it's time to analyze and evaluate your contacts so you can see the types of people on your list. There are different types of people in the world who have varying degrees of influence over others, which can have a real impact on the expansion of your business.

Influencers and Low-Hanging Fruit

From what I have seen over years in this industry, people who perform at the highest level in direct sales or MLM are those who have also had success with something else in the past. It is usually someone who is already performing at a high level in another arena, i.e., athletes, business owners, competitors, record breakers, entrepreneurs—motivated, driven people who have achieved success at some point in their lives that usually do well in this industry even if they have never done anything like this before.

Successful people typically look at things differently than the average person. They're not tied to doing business "as usual"; they look beyond the status quo and are usually open to more creative avenues that can expand their horizons either professionally or personally. They have the ability to create new ideas and concepts, and are often more willing to accept new challenges. They often veer from the traditional path and think outside the box. They also rely on their education, whether it's comprised of traditional schooling or gained through real-world experience.

That said, people who haven't had *any* prior success can still be successful in direct sales or network marketing. By comparison, people who have their own personal motivation and who build from a proven track record will perform at a higher level, recruit more prospects and bring more to the table than the average person in this industry. In my business, I call these people "influencers"; they can also be referred to as "pillars of the community." Everyone knows them and respects them, they inform and persuade others and they are often the voice for those around them. These are people like the heads of the PTA, mayors, local business owners, politicians, police chiefs, school principals, celebrities, bankers, head soccer moms, or anyone else who assumes the role of making choices for a group and who is viewed as a well-known decision maker. **Successful people are influencers** most of the time because they are viewed as experts in their field or niche. This also gives them credibility among their social circle, which can lead to finding and attracting more influencers. You can literally grow a huge customer base or organization by focusing on influencers.

One of my favorite business books is "The Tipping Point" by Malcolm Gladwell. In this book, Gladwell explains different characteristics people have that lead a concept or idea to a tipping point. The people I call "influencers" are almost a hybrid of the different types of people he talks about in his book. I recommend when you finish this book you read "The Tipping Point." It will give you a much better understanding of the psychology behind why ideas hit "tipping points," which in business means massive customer adoption. I honestly believe you can start with one or two influencers and can create an unbelievable business for yourself, accelerating your overall success through rapid growth of your network and faster adoption of your products and ideas based on the amount of influence these people possess.

I can point to several instances when bringing in just *one* of these types of people completely changed someone's business in this industry. The problem is most people generally tend to pursue what is known as "low-hanging fruit." In my opinion these types of prospects are those who are comfortable to talk to and who are easy to influence. People like your kid brother or sister, your childhood sidekick, your unemployed neighbor, your best friend or your friend who has joined eight network marketing companies before, and who will sign up for anything. Now, I don't want to generalize too much here. Everyone has the ability to succeed and these contacts can very well be the spark you need in your business; however, this is *usually* not the case. Yet, nine times out of 10, this is where most people start recruiting. As a result, they build their team from people who do not have what it takes to really connect with people, who are not "influencers" and who have a harder time getting other people to come on board and trust them.

Guess what happens when someone who lacks credibility tries to influence others? They don't get the results they want. And because of their own self-imposed limitations, lack of charisma or anything else that undermines their ability to reach other people, they can't get others to see the world from their point of view. Eventually they lose sight of why they started in the first place which leads them to quit or become uninspired or disinterested in their business. If you work closely with these people and they edify you properly, you can get involved and help them influence others; but, generally speaking, they will not have a high level of success, especially when they are working alone.

Recruit Up

Don't make the mistake of limiting your recruiting efforts to "low-hanging fruit." When you pitch the product and the business opportunity, let the prospect decide whether he or she would like to be a customer or a distributor. By all means, give everyone the chance to decide how they want to participate and at what level. But you should also be thorough, and corral as many "influencers" as possible. You have to "Recruit Up." If you go after your *best* prospects first, you'll have a higher level of success, and more importantly, a *much* higher chance of having *huge* success long-term. "Recruiting Up" means going after the people on the top of your list, and targeting your best prospects who have "influencer" characteristics.

Successful people are influencers

So, how do you recruit up? It all comes down to who you know. It helps if you start off by thinking about who you want to bring into your business and work backwards. Who do you know that is an influencer? Or, whom do you know in your circles that has relationships or can introduce you to the person of influence? Recruiting up could come down to just two introductions. For example, recently I sat down with a new team member and as we evaluated her list, I noticed she didn't have very many "influencers" on it. So I began to ask her questions about the people who were on her list, and it turned out that her mother worked in the Mayor's office with several high-ranking officials. Although my new recruit didn't know any of the people her mother worked with, I immediately had her schedule a meeting with her mom, who we signed up, and this opened the door to some of the most powerful people in her community.

As the size of your team grows, step back and figure out how to leverage the connections you have built so far. Ask yourself, for instance, who on your team can introduce you to the influencers in your community? After personally recruiting celebrities, top business owners and every type of highly successful person imaginable, I am firmly convinced that it is just a matter of finding the right connection who will make the introduction that can open doors to the success you are seeking. Sometimes a person on your team can introduce you directly to the type of person you are trying to meet and at other times someone on your team will lead you to the person who can make that introduction for you with just one phone call.

The Chicken List

Everyone knows someone who can make introductions to "influencers" in the community, but, for whatever reason, we either wait to talk to them until we have already had some level of success building our business or we *never* talk to them at all! This is what I call the "Chicken List"—a list of people who are successful, proven, connected, powerful and influential and who could unlock your entire business, but you are too scared to approach them or you are too intimidated to share your concept with them.

Maybe you've heard this before. Maybe this is just another example of how, when you get out of your own way, you can create the results you want. But listen: this is not just an abstract concept, a "you-should" idea to store for later! It's crucial that you understand just how powerful your "Chicken List" can be. It's also important to recognize that every day you coach and pour energy into the "low-hanging fruit," is a day you delay your ultimate success. And while it's easy to talk to people who are not intimidating or who don't have many options, please realize that for the most part these people will not be the ones responsible for lighting your business on fire. What it comes down to is this: anytime you use your "Chicken List," you usually "Recruit Up," and recruiting up can have a tremendous effect on your business.

Look for this pattern in your team immediately: Someone has brought in new recruits, but they are not getting any duplication. In other words, the people they are asking to become part of the company are not getting any results or are achieving very little. If this occurs inside your organization, the members of your team probably have a *very big* "Chicken List." In most cases, "Chicken

List" contacts perform very well, establishing early success, requiring little support or guidance and, in turn, recruiting high-quality, motivated and self-sufficient members.

I usually have this talk with someone when they are fairly new to my business. I will sit down with them and ask questions like:

- "If you were starting a billion-dollar company who would you have on your board of directors?"

- "Who, among people you respect and look up to, would you use as a business advisor?"

- "Who is the most successful person you know?"

- "Who is the wealthiest person you know?"

These questions can either pinpoint the exact individuals the prospect needs to talk to, or, at the very least, trigger them to begin thinking about the right types of people who can help grow their business. These questions will definitely help if you have a team member who doesn't realize just how big their "Chicken List" really is. A brainstorming session will give your new associate an added level of confidence in their ability to bring influencers into the business, and it will also give you a chance to scout the type of talent they have in their network.

This can also help you determine if your new team member is on the right track, and identify if they will become a potential superstar you can pour your energy into. If they are an influencer, you will also want to know if they can connect you to another person who is similar to themselves. People generally spend time and associate with people who are like-minded and have comparable backgrounds or interests in the people who will be on their own list. When you start getting the contacts on someone's "Chicken List," there's an excellent likelihood that the people on their list will have more high-quality contacts just like them!

Here are a few phrases I use when approaching or contacting prospects on the "Chicken List":

- "I really respect your opinion, and I would like you to look at this."

- "I have always admired your success and I would appreciate your feedback on something I am working on."

- "It would mean so much to me to have someone with your level of success analyze this."

The idea is not to beg or sound needy, but to give them the respect they deserve and put them in a place where you can edify them, and then ask them to consider listening to the business opportunity or seeing the products. Those who have achieved success in their lives have had people who have helped them along the way, so when someone else asks them for feedback and support they usually have no problem returning the favor. Successful people didn't do it on their own; they have all had mentors or teachers, so if you come from a position of respect for them and their achievements they will generally take a look at what you are doing.

You may find that some people on your "Chicken List" have ITC or the "I'm Too Cool" disease. If you haven't heard this term before, it is basically a way to describe someone who thinks they are too cool for Network Marketing or

Those who have achieved success in their lives have had people who have helped them along the way.

Direct Sales. Usually this is created by a misconception or a lack of knowledge by someone who is probably knowledgeable in other areas. Because of what they know, they believe they are also just as knowledgeable outside their area of expertise. However, that's usually not the case, especially when it comes to your company or products. It is important that you address someone like this with the help of your upline if you are new to your business. It can deflate your confidence to deal with people with preconceived notions about your business. If you don't have the luxury of asking your upline or someone else from your team for help, then my best advice is to just kill them with kindness and take whatever criticisms they give you with the understanding that they probably do not understand your industry, your company or your products. Tell them you respect their opinion and you value their input and continue to build up their ego, and if they decide that it is not for them you have absolutely nothing to lose. If you give them respect and speak to them professionally, you never know, they might just open up and decide to listen. I have had several people who I have continued to share my knowledge with, people who started off with this attitude and because I was respectful to them, they eventually warmed up to what I had to say about my company and products.

With this practice, I have been able to recruit celebrities and professional athletes who would definitely fall on most people's "Chicken List." Many people would be intimidated or reluctant to approach this level of prospect, and although they may not actually work your business, having them in your organization can do wonders to your credibility, allowing you to attract more "Chicken List" contacts. When successful and accomplished people hear about how other people they have a great deal of respect for like the products or became part of an opportunity you are promoting, it is easier to get them to take a look and to ultimately participate at some level.

What's interesting is that most people either know a celebrity or professional athlete or know someone who does. Yet, most people will never approach them with their product or concept because they don't feel like they need it. One thing I have learned is that most celebrities and professional athletes have a *very limited* window on their career and peak earning years. Most of them understand this, and are possibly even concerned about it. What's more, you have a solution for them to create an additional revenue stream, and also help them identify what their exit strategy can be when their career comes to an end. So when it comes down to it, couldn't they actually be the perfect prospect?

Depending on your level of success, and your track record, I advise asking your upline for support when you find someone who has access to this level of prospect. That way, you can introduce them to someone who has achieved the level of success you will want them to visualize for themselves. At that point, other than answering specific concerns they may have about endorsements or their image, I would proceed with them the same way I would with any prospect. Keep the message exactly the same. This is exactly how to handle people on your "Chicken List." If you place them on a pedestal or feed their ego too much, you will only put distance between you and them, which ultimately makes them very difficult to recruit. Another common mistake made with celebrities and professional athletes is to over promise on the work you will do for them. This sets up an insurmountable expectation. While it's nice to have them on your team, it doesn't help if they expect you to do everything. It's better, by far, if you refer to the opportunity as a partnership and talk about expectations in line with mutual benefit, mutual cooperation and effort. I have found that people who place their contacts on pedestals often slow down their level of success because they're providing special treatment to their prospects individually, and the amount of work involved becomes counter-productive. So, while you may be two introductions away from attracting powerful "influencers" into your business, make sure you explain the contributions required from both parties in the initial meeting because they could be the exact contact responsible for opening up a whole new realm of possibilities for your future.

I encourage you to stop at this point and rebuild your list. Make sure you add all the names from your "Chicken List"—people you think may be too successful, too rich, too busy or not interested in your business, products or services.

Casting a Wide Net

Of course, your hit list will not just contain influencers, but also anyone else you can think of because, remember, you're looking for anyone who knows you, likes you or trusts you. You need to broaden your list to include everyone who fits within this category. The biggest mistake most people make is trying to predetermine who they think will buy or join before they ever speak to them. My experience has taught me one thing more than anything else: "You never know who is going to succeed in your business and you never know who will purchase your products." **Therefore you want to cast the widest net possible. Include everyone you possibly can to make your overall opportunity that much bigger.**

I marvel at the number of people who tell me when they start in network marketing that they would rather talk to people they don't know rather than to people they do know. This is a very telling sign of why people struggle in this industry, because it shows that they don't want to feel like they've failed in front of someone they know. In other words, if they present the product to someone who tells them "no," they feel like they've failed at something in front of a person whose opinion matters to them. However, nothing could be further from the truth. This misconception stems from the belief that people feel like they have to "sell" to someone they know or care about. In my opinion, if you believe in your company, products or services, you owe it to your friends, family and associates to at least let them know what you're doing regardless of whether or not they decide to purchase or participate. Do you want them to see your success down the road and then have them ask, "Why didn't you think of me?" I would rather have people tell me "no" than to have them later insinuate that I thought they weren't good enough, couldn't afford it, or had some other reason for not sharing the opportunity with them in the first place. I've also had several people tell me "no" in the beginning, who have come back later after seeing my success, and get on board. This is the beauty of casting a wide net, and sharing the opportunity with as many people as you can, because even if someone doesn't choose to participate as a customer or distributor right off the bat, you never know how they might benefit your business in the future.

I often get asked, "What if I don't know anyone?" or "What if I don't have anyone to talk to?" This comes up often when people have relocated to a new area. How can they build a local market in addition to working their previous market virtually? I am convinced I could relocate to any city in the world, sell my products or services and build a team of customers and distributors in a matter of weeks. The most important part of this to remember is the phrase, "I believe I can." The people who feel like they don't know anyone and, by extension, don't have anyone to talk to, are operating from a limiting belief that is simply not true.

We were born with a need to socialize and interact with others. That's why we're so advanced as a species. People want to interact with others, and, in my opinion, it is *impossible* for someone to *not know anyone*! So, do something that comes natural and follow the design of your behavior—be social and build your business at the same time you're living your everyday life. Believe me, you can build a huge team and business without spending a *dime* on advertising, even if you feel like your warm market is not ideal or you feel like it's been depleted. Over the last six years, I've lived in four different cities, and each time I've moved, I've started a new team with absolutely no advertising. That makes this industry and this type of business the lowest overhead business model you could possibly find! Low overhead is one of the things that makes this industry so amazing. It levels the playing field for anyone to get involved for very little initial capital! You can start a business in this industry with very minimal investment and no real long-term overhead, and continue to grow your business no matter where you're located. When you go into your market knowing you'll succeed, and knowing it's just a matter of time until you have a team, then you're well on your way to a high level of success.

Be Active and Authentic

One of the most important parts of starting a market from scratch is being active. Not physically active, although that will probably help you as well, but active in the community where you intend to start your team. Being active can be as simple as going to your to your local gym, grocery store or restaurant. There are always opportunities to prospect, especially in a society where most of our social interaction is channeled through technology, rather than personal, face-to-face communication. People are looking for personal human interaction when they get out of their homes. It's easier than ever to strike up conversations wherever you go, especially local places where it's essential to visit with people around you. Whenever you're out and about, be mindful of your business and your products. Watch for opportunities to meet people and take this rule to heart: Friends first, recruit later. Don't dominate conversations. Ask questions and pay attention to the answers. The answers will guide you in your quest for establishing a strong connection that will help you communicate with them more affectively. Be open, friendly and engaging. Most of all, be genuine. When you're authentic, people will share more, care more and establish a vested interest in your cause, when you decide to share it with them.

Give yourself an opportunity to learn about the person you're talking to. Take your time. Remember, this is your chance to figure out if they can be a potential customer or prospect. If you start off the conversation by asking them simple questions, they'll usually engage in the conversation by asking you questions in return. Find a reason to talk to them such as a common interest or use a conversation starter to allow you to get to know the person.

For example, I was recently at the airport and a well-dressed couple was sitting next to me on the rental car shuttle, and they happened to have a small son about the age of my daughter. I turned to them and asked, "How old is your son?" I then said I have a daughter about the same age, and they, of course, asked me how old she was and that developed into a conversation where I wound up getting their contact information so I could follow up with them later. I did this by explaining that I often do business in their area and that I would like to look them up next time I was in town for advice on where to eat and what sights to see. It was as simple as that!

You have to step out of your comfort zone a little and start some conversations. Whenever I move to a new place, I make it a point to get out on the town and meet people at the mall, restaurants, stores and local businesses. One of my mentors collects people's information wherever he goes. It's amazing to watch him in action. We used to have competitions on who could get the most business cards when we went out. He used the "three-foot-rule," meaning, anytime he gets within three feet of someone he introduces himself and finds creative reasons to strike up a conversation with them.

Many people over-think how to recruit new contacts and they tend to scare them off when they're prospecting. They are too sales-y, and talk about their products or services as soon as they meet them, and that turns most people off. Instead, why not create small talk, which builds a relationship first and then find a reason to introduce your products or services to them at a later time? It's easier to work your business or products into the conversation later or when the opportunity presents itself. Then the person feels like it is brought up on "their" terms, and was not forced on them.

The Follow-Up

Regardless of whether you are working with your "hit list" or prospecting in your local area, you need to become a professional networker. To do so, it's important to organize your information and have a system for follow-up. Follow-up is one of the weakest skills for most networkers. So, if you want to be above average, you need to master systematic follow-up.

The sooner you follow up, the more likely your prospect will remember you and the interaction they had with you. Having a good system of how you follow up is crucial to your success in strengthening relationships and the likelihood of turning prospects into customers or distributors. Strike while the iron is hot! I use the iPhone application "The Mobile Networker" to stay organized, and this is the system I use when I am following up with new prospects:

1. I enter their contact information into my phone immediately, even if they give me a business card. I will do this on the spot and send them a text while they are standing there with my information, if we have time. I also never carry cards on me so it gives me the perfect excuse to ask for their card or information and I put it right into my phone.

2. I put notes about everything we talked about during our conversation in the notes section of my phone. I do this while it is fresh on my mind, and sometimes I do this while I am actually sitting and talking to them.

3. I send them a follow-up email or text about how nice it was to meet with them, or a thank-you for chatting with me. I try to leave the door open for future conversations when I send the email or text by saying "I look forward to catching up with you again soon." If I found something out about their business or what they do I will mention "I would like to hear more about your business," or "I would like to chat business with you sometime and see if we can help each other."

4. I will then follow back up with them on a live call within 48 hours of the first meeting and try to set up a time to either meet them for coffee or lunch, or if things have progressed enough I will try to invite them to one of our live events.

The key is following up quickly and being able to remember the conversation you had with them so you can continue to build rapport and trust. This way it will not sound like you are just trying to sell or recruit them.

Everything we have discussed in this chapter is designed to get your business going regardless of how much experience you have in this industry. Since we covered so many approaches, along with the different people you will interact with, it is important that you sit down and look at your business in order to figure out which approach and type of people you need to add to your business. You can also go through the different scenarios we have discussed individually with people on your team, because I promise you, most people have a *very large* "Chicken List" that they are not taking advantage of currently.

Whether you are truly starting from scratch or you just feel like you need a fresh start, the information we covered in this chapter is the foundation to creating your business, step-by-step.

3

The First 48

I travel the world extensively, providing training for my
organization and my company, and one of the questions I get
asked most often by new representatives at trainings is: "What
should I do with a new person?" Many top performers spend a lot
of time educating their teams of distributors about how to obtain
more sales and more volume, which is important to growing their
business. But recognize, also, that sales and recruitment make up
only half the battle. Recruitment covers most aspects of the
business until the customer actually signs up, but then what do you
do with them once they sign up? What's your game plan after you
bring someone into your organization? I feel like leaders also need
to train their teams on what to do *after* you have added a customer
to your team. Actually, this should be a prerequisite to sales and
recruitment, because without understanding this concept your
team members may not be around long enough to use everything
else we talk about later in the book. That said, one of the biggest
problems new representatives come across is retention. How do
you retain customers, distributors and representatives? From my
experience, it's clear that many people don't know what to do after
they initially sign up or purchase products in this industry. In this
chapter, I will explain my process for working with new people; but
first, I feel it's important to discuss the psychology of a new person,
because unless you understand their mindset and their challenges,
you cannot work with them effectively.

Psychology of a New Representative/Customer

If you want to influence the way someone thinks, or affect their actions you must understand the "why" behind their behavior. It is important to comprehend the psychology of prospective customers during the sales process and, of course, immediately following the sales process, so you can effectively build your business. In general, there will be two main thoughts someone will have when they are introduced to your company, products or presentation for the first time:

1. **"Does this work?"** This question focuses on the products and the results of the products. It reflects the attitude and mindset people have as they try to determine if this product or service is right for them: Is it believable? Is there proof/documentation? What is the documentation? Does it seem realistic? These questions are usually answered by facts, research, testimonials, before-and-after proof, and additional information that can help someone see the results and understand that success is possible and that the company can back up what they are saying.

2. **"Can I do this?"** When someone asks themselves, "Can I do this?" it reflects the personal conflict they must overcome to be able to join your program or purchase your products. Internal questions such as: "Can I do what they are doing right now? What is the system? What is the program? Which types of people are having success? Are these people like me? Are these results possible for me? Does it seem easy? Do I have enough experience to be good at this?" These questions are solved by anticipating and answering doubts and concerns as you go through your entire presentation. Try to ensure the information you cover answers these questions as you share your message. If these fears or obstacles are overcome in the information you present, the person should be ready to join you at the end of the presentation. These questions are normally answered by making the presentation simple and easy to

understand, showing a system for achieving results, illustrating results from people in similar positions, talking about support and assistance, and making it seem possible for the average person to have some level of success.

If you can successfully answer these questions when you share your program, you are going to build a large base of customers and representatives. This is the beginning of the psychological process that you must understand to attract and retain new members. Once new members feel comfortable enough with the information you have shared, and they have made a commitment to get involved at some level, they will go through a roller coaster of emotions that will dictate their success with the program. I find it fascinating that something like running your own business, or trying a new product or program can elicit such heightened emotions and feelings from people. This emotional roller coaster begins as soon as they sign on the dotted line. If you are effective at managing expectations and can help stabilize their reactions, you will have success beyond your greatest expectations.

48 Hours to Success

The number one way to keep the roller coaster moving in the right direction is for the person to have success as soon possible. There is no better cure for an emotional roller coaster than immediate success. No matter how much negativity your new customers or representatives face, if they have had success, it will go in one ear and right out the other. It is almost as if success gives your new people a shield to deflect any negativity and protect them from any obstacles that get in their way. Therefore, one of my main goals with a new person is for them to have immediate success, somehow, someway!

Success breeds success, and longevity. Immediate success is crucial for someone to succeed long-term in your business. Whether it's experiencing immediate results from your products and services or it's achieving success with your business, your main short-term goal is for a new representative or member to have some type of success. This is why I put so much emphasis on the first 48 hours after they join. So many things can happen in the first few days after coming on board, and it is **absolutely** crucial that you engage immediately with your new people before that window closes. Understand that people will continue to have doubts and second guess themselves after they join, especially those who have never done anything like this before. As a result, what generally happens after they join is that they will head straight to their most valued friends and family with **no training**, and no education on the products or services and they will try to get second opinions about their new endeavor. Now keep in mind, the people they are talking to have probably not heard of the company, have probably not seen the product or service before, and, what's more, they may have negative preconceived ideas that stem from other experiences. In short, all of these things can be just enough to discourage your new person before they ever get started. I have seen this happen over and over again: a person who just joined went home and talked to their spouse or significant other and that person discouraged them and they ended up cancelling their order or asking for a refund.

If you want to influence the way someone thinks, you must understand the "why" behind their behavior.

When I was new in the industry, this happened to me pretty regularly because I didn't understand the psychology and process that a new person goes through as soon as they get involved. However, once I understood their mindset, their fears and anxieties, my business changed dramatically. Not only did I see more immediate results, I also had a much higher retention rate of new customers and representatives. Just having this awareness is the greatest weapon you could possibly have against attrition in your organization. Realize that those who are new to your company will be extremely excited and they may want to shout it from the mountain tops that they have found a way to change their life either through a new product or service or by earning exciting income. This is positive—you don't want to crush their dream, but realize they have no training or knowledge other than what they just heard in a brief overview. So what can you do to keep these new people who have no training or experience from going home and hurting their business before they ever get started? Give them hope. Let them know that you will provide them with a personal plan to help them achieve the results that they are looking for, and let them know it is very important that they *do not* try to do anything on their own *until* they have that plan in place. This is why that 48-hour window is so important. New members want to see immediate results, and they are so excited that they will go out there and try to talk to everyone they know if you don't give them any direction. So, as soon as someone joins my team, I say the following to them:

> *"I am so excited you have joined our company, and I am going to share our system with you so you can achieve the results you are looking for. We are going to create a custom plan for you to achieve results immediately. However, it is very important that until we meet and create this plan that you do not try to do this on your own. I have been doing this for a while and I will be able to tell you exactly what to do and what **not** to do so that you do not make the same mistakes that I did when I started. Let's meet as soon as possible to go over this plan. Are you available to meet for coffee tomorrow morning? In the meantime, please just try to think about all of the things that you would like to gain from our product and our opportunity, and we will work on exactly how to do that when we meet tomorrow."*

This is not going to keep everyone from going and collecting second opinions from everyone they know, but I do believe if you have this session scheduled with them immediately, they will say to themselves, "Well we are meeting tomorrow so I can wait at least another day until I find out everything I need to know." The goal is to contain their excitement until you meet with them the next day. When I teach this system to my team, I tell them that it is CRITICAL to do this meeting in the first 48 hours, but I always try to do it in the first 24 hours if at all possible. The less time they have to try to do it on their own without any training or direction, the less likely they will be to have a bad experience with someone who is negative. The reason why new people are more susceptible to negativity is because they are not educated enough to explain the products or services fully, and answer questions that people will ask them. If you explain what I shared with you in the paragraph above, the new person will contain their enthusiasm and at the same time will have something to look forward to that will keep them focused on their new goals instead of trying to do it all on their own.

The Game Plan Session

Now that you have a meeting scheduled with your new person, preferably the day after signing them up, let's discuss what should happen during that very important first session. You should have a Game Plan Session with your new customers, not just your new representatives who are serious about working with the business. If you want to retain your customers, creating a game plan for them on how to use the products or services can be equally as important to your businesses long-term success and especially to your residual income. Obviously creating a game plan for a customer to make sure they know how to use the products or services properly is a totally different meeting than the meeting you will have with someone who is looking to make money with the opportunity. Here are some things to cover with a new customer who is not interested in pursuing the opportunity:

- Ask what their goals are with the products and services.
- Show them how to use the products or services.
- Create a plan for them to get the results that they want to achieve based on the goals they have previously stated.
- Create a calendar or a timeline that will allow them to monitor their results or track their progress.
- Share important company information that will help them use the products or services more effectively.

- Create an accountability plan for them so you can help monitor their results.

Your main objective during a Game Plan Session for a new customer is to familiarize them with everything they need to know to get the most out of your products and services. If you can go through all of the features and benefits as the products relate to their personal goals they will become a loyal customer. Make sure they have everything they need in order to be able to re-order or add other products or services to their initial order. You should also keep a record of their goals and objectives so you can follow up with them on their progress at a later time.

The Game Plan Session I have with someone who is interested in making money and working the business is *completely* different than the session I would have with someone who only wants to be a customer. Members who have monetary goals are not as focused on getting results with the products or the services. Veterans reading this book right now might understand that being a fan of your product and incorporating it into your everyday life is important, and that is very true. However, if someone is focused on making money and that is their main objective, then it is crucial that they have immediate success in that area or they will get discouraged very, very quickly. They will integrate the products and services as they become more familiar with the program, but do not spend your entire Game Planning Session explaining everything about products, services, company history, back office technology, order forms, websites and things that do not create an immediate paycheck for them. They will have plenty of opportunities to learn these things if they are still in your business a month from now.

If you don't allow someone to experience immediate success, they may not be here a month from now, which makes understanding the intricacies of your business and product line completely irrelevant. I have not always followed this school of thought on initial Game Planning Sessions with new members. I used to do exactly what I am telling you NOT to do, and this is where experience comes in. What I noticed was that my new members

Success breeds success! were very educated on products and services, but they were not getting immediate monetary results and my team was not growing as fast as I wanted it to. So, I started focusing on helping my team get immediate monetary results and my business went to a whole new level. This is what I do in my Game Planning Session with my new representatives today, and this is what has generated thousands of customers around the world. I suggest you cover the following for new representatives that are focused on promoting your business:

1. What are your goals?

If you do not know what they are trying to achieve, it's impossible to customize a plan for them that they will stick with. If they only want to make a few hundred dollars a month, their plan and schedule will look completely different from someone who wants to make several thousand a month. I used to make the mistake of assuming everyone wanted to make six figures a month like I did, which is simply not the case. You must find out exactly what your new member wants to achieve to be able to develop a plan they feel is congruent with the lifestyle they want to achieve. This is also the time when I set proper expectations about how results will occur for them in this industry. In a typical job, people are used to working and getting paid immediately for the time they put in; but this industry is different. Generally the work you put in today will not show up on your paycheck for about three to six months from today. Why? Because this industry is not based on sales, it is based on duplication. Duplication is not a fast process, *especially* at the beginning because there are not as many people doing the work. When a new member starts, there is *only one* person on their team, so any results that are achieved are the product of one individual. Once they follow the program for at least 60-90 days, they will have more people contributing to the overall success of their organization. As their business grows, results will show up down the road because the people they share this with today will start to get their own results and grow their own teams. If you explain this to your new people, they will NOT get stuck in the "Get Rich Quick" mentality. I constantly remind people "What you are doing today will pay you three to six months from now."

2. What is your schedule like?

You cannot create a work schedule for someone if you do not know what their current commitments are. You can explain the level of work that is required to achieve the results they want, but how you work that activity into their calendar depends on what their typical day looks like. You may have someone who is taking night classes, for instance, or who works in the evenings, so they may not be able to attend your traditional evening meetings like the majority of your team. In that case, you will have to customize a game plan and schedule that fits with their commitments and the amount of time they are willing to spend on the business. After I understand what a new representative's commitments are, I will put a calendar together for them. This will give them a consistent schedule that they can maintain weekly. I will also usually schedule their "Grand Opening" during this session so that I can get them off to a fast start; this entails explaining to them in detail about how to do a "Grand Opening." We will cover this when we discuss events later in the book. But for now, just make sure your new member understands what they must do in order to achieve the results they are looking for. This is all about managing someone's expectations. Setting proper expectations during this part of the Game Plan Session is a great way to hold them accountable, because they commit to their assignments and responsibilities based on *their* goals not *yours*.

3. Get their list

This is where the real work of the Game Plan Session begins. If you skip this step, you will lose an opportunity to find out the types of people they have on their list, thereby leaving the types of people they are going to contact to chance. This is what I say to help identify the best people on their list:

"Imagine you had an invention that was going to revolutionize the world, and to build your invention you needed $10 million. An investor agrees to give you the money, on one condition: You must recruit a board of directors that the investor would approve of. So you have to choose your best 10 people to sit on your board of directors in order to get the funding. Look at your list. Who are the 10 most successful people you know who you would contact to sit on your board?"

This gets people thinking about the right types of people that we want to introduce to our business. We will talk about the different types of prospects and personalities in other chapters in the book, but the main objective is to get to their *best* 10 people first. I will also make a copy of the list so that I can ensure my new representative is working their list properly. I will follow up with them and ask about each person on the list after the initial Game Planning Session.

4. Make the calls

Once you have the top 10 list let your new member know that they must start inviting the people on their list immediately. This is the biggest mistake new people make when they are doing their Game Planning Sessions with new people. Your new members will often be hesitant to make the calls while you sit there and watch them go through the process. If this is the case, explain why it is important that they do it now so that you can help them through the process. This also keeps them from returning home and procrastinating, which will cause you to lose your precious 48-hour window to achieve results. Teach them the simple two-step invite. I cover this in more detail later in the book, but you need it for this step:

- Are you free tomorrow at 7:30?

- **If yes:** "Can you meet me at the coffee shop, I have something I want you to see." **If no:** "It's OK, we'll catch up later."

This makes it simple and also keeps people from asking a lot of questions. Tell your new member that if their prospect asks questions, to say the following: "It's very important to me and I need you to meet me." Let your new member know that they can, of course, do this invite by text message if that's how they commonly communicate with their friends and contacts. The rule of thumb is to communicate how they would normally communicate; so, if they text their contact regularly, then tell them to text the invite; and if they call them regularly, then tell them to call and invite them. Let them know that they can substitute the location and time of the meeting to correspond with the **next available** event. Last-minute invites are the best. If they can help it, tell them to not invite their prospect to something that happens a week from now. If an event doesn't occur in the next 48 hours, then they can schedule them individually as long as they have a website, DVD or other presentation that they can show their prospect when they meet with them. The other option you have is to schedule a "Grand Opening" for them in the next 48 hours, and you can follow my blueprint for that type of event in the chapter "There's an Event for That."

I have discovered that the most important thing you can accomplish in this Game Planning Session is to create initial results through activity. If you do the first three steps, but you do not do step four, then your Game Planning Session has been a waste of time. Your new representative needs to see light at the end of the tunnel, and having their prospects scheduled for some type of exposure keeps them from going out there and trying to explain the business to everyone on their own without the proper environment. If this activity happens immediately, and they make that **first sale**, then you have just increased their chance for long term success substantially. Now all you have to do is keep them on the path of continued success and you have just created one of your future superstars.

Tell, Show, Try, Do

One of my mentors explained it to me best, "If you want someone to have immediate results, you have to "Tell, Show, Try, Do." If you can do all four of these steps with a new person in their first 48 hours you will create a culture of success inside your organization. The mistake most new people make is they usually only do the first component with most of their new people. Most people think that if they tell someone to do something that they will automatically just do exactly as they say, but the reality is that most people "do as they see, not as they are told." If you want them to have a successful first 48 hours, you must complete each one of the following steps with them:

1. **Tell:** This is generally the easiest step for most people because it is simple and we have been doing it all of our lives. This step is easy we just tell people exactly what they need to do in order to have success. It sounds simple enough, but the problem with this step is that it is only effective if you follow it up with the other three components. It is very important that you walk your new people through exactly what they should do immediately to be successful. Don't focus on telling them what to do a month from now or two months from now; just focus on what they should do in the immediate future to achieve results.

2. **Show:** For most people, this step is the hardest. It's much easier to tell someone what to do than it is to show them what to do. In my opinion this step shouldn't amount to just providing them with an example of what to do. You have to actually DO exactly what you are telling them to do; in other words, they need to *see* you do it yourself. Lead by example. Remember, they have probably never done anything like this before in their life, and they may be nervous and apprehensive about most aspects of the business. You can calm their nerves and overcome their fears by showing them an example of someone else being successful. This

means you should constantly be an example for your team and, most importantly, for your new people. Do the things you are telling your people to do, because if you are only saying it and not actually doing it yourself, they will eventually stop listening to you. If you are not actively inviting in the market you are working in, then try to have someone who is getting results come in and let the new person observe what they are doing that is working for them. This will ensure they have an example of exactly what they should be doing. Bottom line: your new member will feel more comfortable doing it themselves if they can see someone else doing it successfully first.

3. **Try:** Once a new person sees someone go through the process that they are supposed to be doing themselves, it is time for them to give it a try. It is very important that you observe this activity take place. That way, you'll be able to correct mistakes, and compliment them on their efforts and reinforce their positive behavior. This is the step that, if left out, scares me the most. How could you let your people go out there and try to do the business without having an idea about what they are actually doing? The only way to know if your people are doing things properly is to watch them perform. If you are not present, follow up with them and ask them very detailed questions about their activities or ask them to role play with you about how the interaction took place. Of course, the only way to know for sure if your people are on the right track is to watch them in action.

4. **Do:** This is the most natural of the steps because it is the product of successful implementation of the first three steps. If you do the first steps properly with your new people, they will feel empowered, supported and confident as they start working the business on their own. This is where they simply start doing exactly what you have taught them to do. How do you know if you did the first three steps properly? A good indicator is if your people are getting results while they are working alone. If your members are

not staying active or achieving success on their own, that's a sign that you need to start back with them at step one.

Your job as a leader is to set the pace for your team, and to lead by example. Following these four steps will let your people know that you will do the work alongside them. Some new leaders only accomplish step number one and tell their people what to do, but they never actually do it themselves. If you don't do what you are asking your people to do, and let them see you follow the same steps, they will doubt you and do it their own way; or worse, they won't do anything at all. These four steps are crucial to use for new people getting started, but they also give you a blueprint for teaching other new concepts to your team. You can use this technique to help teach your leaders and superstars advanced skills like presenting and training with this exact same method.

The Quitting Threshold

The Game Plan Session is designed to get someone to have immediate results within the **first 48 hours** of joining, and to eliminate the possibility of the new member trying to do everything on their own. Now that you have created some initial success with your new representative by following this program, you have also increased their overall chances of achieving all of their long-term goals. However, initial success does NOT guarantee long-term success so you still have work to do. The first few weeks someone is in your business will be an emotional roller coaster for them, like we have discussed. It will be filled with the ups and downs of starting a new adventure and running their own business. They will still have to face **doubters** and they will still have **challenges**, even if you get them off to a fast start. Moving forward, your job is to keep them off the "Line" that I call "The Quitting Threshold." The quitting threshold exists for everyone; it exists for your top performers just as it exists for your new team members. It is your job to always know where your people are in regards to that "Line." The reason I call it a "Line" is because once they cross it, they are going to quit.

Network Marketing is easy to get into, and it's also generally easy to get out of. If someone quits at Network Marketing, it's probably because they have quit at many things in life. Quitting is the only way you can fail in this industry. Because this is your own business, you cannot fire yourself and the company cannot fire you unless you break the rules. So, someone could be the worst distributor in the history of this industry and they still cannot be fired. That means that you should make a commitment to yourself **not to quit**, and tell yourself you **WILL** be here five years from now. Most people out there may say that they will be here five years from now, but in reality they will not make it that far. You cannot take it personally when people decide to quit your business. It's going to happen, because the barrier to entry into your business is very low compared to starting a traditional business.

Give them hope! You don't have to be a rocket scientist to know what the divorce rate is in our country, and just look at the thousands of people who do not finish college. People are quitting things around us every day. The easier it is to quit at something the higher the failure percentage will be. For this reason it is important for you to stay focused on keeping your team intact as long as possible, and the best way to do that is to focus on each individual the best that you can.

If you are aware of where your people are in relationship to the "Line" then you have the power to affect whether they cross that "Line" or not. When you bring on new distributors or customers, think of their time in your business like a piece of sand in an hourglass. When you drop that sand into the top of the hourglass, you only have a certain amount of time until it falls through to the other side, this is just like crossing the "Line." The good thing about THIS hourglass is that you can continually add sand to the top and keep your sand from running out completely on the other side. The way you add "sand" to the life of one of your customers or distributors is to make sure they continue to have more success, more results, hit their goals or feel personal growth. These are the areas of achievement that will keep someone around forever. It takes more than one positive experience to negate a negative one, so if something negative happens to someone on your team, make sure you work with that person closely until you are sure they have had enough positive results to make up for that negative experience.

Throughout this book we are going to focus on activities and concepts that will create positive results for the people inside your organization; however, realize that you have limited time, especially in the beginning, for this process to occur. The less time someone has been in your business, the closer they are to the "Line." In contrast, the longer they have been around and the more success they have experienced, the further away they get from the "Line." Also, remember that just because someone has achieved outstanding results and they have become a leader in your company or your organization does not mean that they cannot cross the "Line." You must constantly be aware of where your people are with their own progress and results, because even though they may seem to be having success, they may not be fulfilled in all areas of their business. As we go through the rest of the book, think about where your people are in regards to the goals they have shared with you in your Game Plan Session. You should continue to have these Game Plan Sessions with people even after their first few weeks so you can evaluate their mindset, their progress, address their setbacks and help them grow personally and professionally. **Be the person that leads them to the success they are searching for!**

4

How to Spell Team

*O*ne thing to keep in mind about your team is the way most people evaluate whether or not you have a true interest in their success is the amount of time you spend with them.. I heard once that "the best way to spell team is T-I-M-E," and that the more time you spend with people, the greater the team bond will become. Friendships forged in this industry are nearly impossible to re-create at other companies outside of this industry. Why? Because relationships formed around the water cooler in an office or along the golf course of a corporate retreat are not the same as those created while helping people re-shape their lives, and reach their full potential. In this industry, a special connection is made between individuals who share similar aspirations, reasons for improving their situation, and who have a thirst for knowledge and personal growth.

These characteristics are so deeply rooted in someone's psychology that when you create memories around those circumstances, they are not easily forgotten. When you truly connect with someone in this industry, you foster trust, you re-affirm belief in what you're doing, and you build friendships *and* partnerships. Helping someone shape their future can create a lasting impression on their character and give them the ability to stay the course through some of the toughest times on their journey. This type of relationship-building is characteristic of someone who is focused on the development of a long-term business and the byproduct of that business, rather than the typical things that contribute to a business like sales, promotions, advancement and bonuses.

Even in the sports world, most leadership development and team building takes place day to day during practice and the time spent off the playing field. It's not what happens during the game and in the heat of battle that forms the bond on most teams, although those events can be incredibly significant. The real bond takes place during the preparation for the main event, and how the team comes together before and after games that creates the connection among team members. The bond is formed during practices, through the sweat and tears, the motivation and hard work tied to perfecting a game plan, the routes, the drills, perfecting routines until everyone gets it right; it's the communication during closed meetings when coaches speak honestly to the team about who they are and what they can become; it's the camaraderie experienced in one-on-ones where players counsel players and coaches guide and mentor their team so they become the leaders they were meant to be.

Your business is no different. The lessons learned and the connections made when there are no customers around are your biggest chances for teaching and team building. Reach out to your people, bring them close, offer them guidance, teach them what you know, share experiences, hear their stories, show them who you are, your gifts, your talents, your challenges, your character and they will be your champions and your greatest assets. In the words of renowned leadership expert and best-selling author John C. Maxwell, "People don't care how much you know, unless they know how much you care."

Over my career I can look back on several trips, banquets, dinners, parties and special moments that have helped create relationships and partnerships I will have for the rest of my life. Although everyday events may appear mundane, they're actually incredible opportunities to share your vision of what is possible through hard work, determination, persistence and ethics. Human interaction is one of the most natural parts of leadership for most people in this industry. Excelling in this area begins with spending time with your team. For some, this is easy because they like being around other people much more than being by themselves. For others, being around their team and business associates on a regular basis may be a struggle or may try their patience, not just from the act of associating with others, but through managing and connecting with others who may have personalities or interests that are dissimilar to their own. The key is to think beyond yourself for the good of your team and your business. When your patience is tested by a challenging team member, consider this: you may be the only person who has ever believed in them. I have returned to this thought many times throughout my career. As I deal with people who have challenging personalities and attitudes, I remind myself to believe in them as if I am the only person who does or ever will. There are numerous leaders and top performers on my team who wouldn't have been as successful in other organizations as they have in my business because they would not have been given time to bloom in their own way.

The majority of the adult workforce is working for someone else's opportunity.

Not only is this useful for an individual and his or her development; it also applies to your team as a whole. Over the last 15 years, I have witnessed events that were turning points for groups I worked with. Some of these were planned by a company or organization, but many were spontaneous developments that created a lasting bond and made a deeper connection. Being part of something bigger than themselves is one of the reasons people get into this industry in the first place. People love participating in a cause that will not only help them, but will also benefit everyone they come in contact with. As they spend time in this industry, they participate in events and share experiences that create memories that will help them overcome obstacles as they pursue their long-term goals. Many of your team members will look back on the memories you created together and draw from the stories they have heard and the lessons they have learned to help them face struggles along the way.

As people age, their belief in themselves slips into a downward spiral. I have heard that by the time we reach our 30s, we have been told, "No", thousands of times. This, among other things as we grow up, takes its toll on our creativity, imagination and belief, and, in turn, changes our perspectives as we transition from children into adults. No wonder, by the time we reach the workforce, we assume that we have to work for someone else, and accept whatever circumstances or situations come our way. America is considered the land of opportunity, yet the majority of the adult workforce is working for someone else's opportunity.

Rest assured, there are ample opportunities for training, bonding and networking with your team. I have made it a point whenever possible to turn everyday tasks into team-building opportunities. If you have to run errands, for instance, why not take a member of your team with you? Take a daily chore and turn it into a way to teach, develop friendship and leadership and create vision. I have taken trips to the mall that wound up being a way to spend quality time with someone and to talk about items or products that catch their eye, helping them understand how to dream bigger and making sure they realize they *deserve* everything they want in life no matter what place they're in. The opportunities you have to spend time with people are perfect to work on limiting beliefs about why they have not achieved the level of success they desire. You can teach them how to think differently, which will open their eyes to bigger and better possibilities. Often I plan these simple activities because I see an opportunity to develop the vision and commitment of one of my future leaders.

For instance, when I was shopping for a new car, I took one of my up-and-coming leaders with me. Shopping for expensive cars is not about ego; it's about bringing people back to the amazing childhood ability to *dream big* and to actually chase those dreams. People get excited about nice things and when they see someone they know and trust in the position to buy, they begin to believe they can achieve the same results. This is one of the best ways to bond with your team. It's just as fun for me as it is for them, and I often wind up learning more about them in the process, which helps me understand myself and others at a deeper level.

Running Buddy

I love animals and I have used my financial success in this industry to purchase several thoroughbred racehorses, which race at different tracks around the United States. Someone shared an interesting, old western tale at a race one time that contains a good lesson for our business. Back in the day, small towns would have horse-pulling contests on the weekends that would function as a form of local entertainment. The contests involved seeing how much weight a horse could pull behind them over a specific distance. Obviously, the horse that pulled the most weight would be the winner. One day a farmer decided to take the top two horses and tie them together and see how much they could pull, and miraculously it wasn't the combined winning weights as one might think, but actually about 20 percent more than what the horses had been able to pull separately. Whether it was physics or psychology, the fact remains that "two heads are better than one."

We can all be more productive if we work together. The first example of working together starts in the purest form between two people who share a common goal or have similar interests. For years, I have trained on the concept of finding a "running buddy" or an accountability partner to work your business with, to help set the tone and pace of your business. This business is not fun to do alone. If I look back over my career at top performers in my company and also top performers in other companies I see very strong partnerships. Maybe not a partnership in the sense that they are sharing their business and their income, but they are working together as a team in most aspects of their business. If you look at the top performers in your company, you will probably notice the same thing. You will see friends, buddies, husband/wife, and even childhood friends who are working together in their business because they have developed a passion for their company or products or they have similar goals, dreams and aspirations.

Cultivating a group dynamic is essential to your business.

You may assume that you need to find someone in your upline or downline to work with, but that's not always the case. If you don't have the luxury of working with someone on your immediate team, there may be someone in your area you might not benefit from financially who will team up with you. In a perfect world, you should try to work with someone on your team, because this can also serve as a development pipeline of future leaders in your organization. The reason this is my preference is because you will both have a financially vested interest in each other's success. This will make the dynamic between the two of you more integrated because you are contributing to each other's financial success. My "running buddies" have changed over the years as people have developed and built large organizations, which in turn, have put them in a position to work with new "running buddies." I have seen some partners work together for years. It's important to find someone with similar goals, ambitions and passions. Your personalities may be different, but if you're moving towards the same goals, you will have similar amounts of commitment. You probably don't want to team up with someone whose goal is to make $500 per month if your goal is to make $50,000 per month. I also think it's OK to work with someone who has a different style or personality than you do because this can help mask individual weaknesses that either one of you may have in running your business. If organization is not your strong point, for instance, then I suggest you team up with someone who is strong in that area. This is just one example of working together to improve the overall production and output of the duo that you will create.

Having a "running buddy" will give you the ability to take each other to a higher level that would not be attained as quickly as working individually. I also use this arena as a sound board for new ideas and goal setting; it can even be a relationship that will help you overcome the ups and downs of the business without negatively affecting the rest of your organization. If you don't currently have a "running buddy," find one as soon as possible. This has been one of my secret weapons through the years, and I think you will multiply your efforts as soon as you make this part of your routine. When you choose a running buddy talk to them about what you want to accomplish, and make sure you get their buy-in before you just assume that they want to be your "running buddy." Also make sure you don't use this as an excuse to offload the work or responsibility on someone else. This should be a mutually beneficial relationship that helps both of your businesses.

Culture

I have always had a special knack for sharing a vision with others, and getting them to see the bigger picture. I believe that vision is the one thing that allows others to believe in themselves and come together for a common goal. Sharing a common goal and having product conviction are core components to creating enthusiastic customers and building culture among team members. Spending time with your team also increases productivity and retention. The key is to **cultivate group culture** based on the identity of your team. If you create a common goal, you'll find ways to tie people together through similar interests.

One of the best ways to secure your future and improve retention inside your organization is to create a team or group culture. The best part is, since it is your team, you can get creative and decide exactly what you want the culture to be like. The first step in creating a team identity or culture can start when you have just a few people on your team. Be warned, however: People who get caught up on group management and not on recruiting new distributors and customers will probably go backwards faster than they went forwards. Do not assume when you start organizing team events and activities your job as a recruiter or representative has changed to manager. Every time I've seen someone put their focus on their team and take it away from their personal business, it is only a matter of time until they experience major attrition. If you primarily act like a manager or boss, your people will start to resent you, or they will begin to think to themselves, "If he or she isn't doing it, then why should I?" You still have to lead by example and set the pace for your team. Along with carrying the torch you must also start to integrate the team concept into your organization.

As we have already discussed, people will often do more for others in a group than they will for themselves. How do you leverage this group dynamic and create a group culture among your team? Start with a group text to highlight hot news and important information for your team. Within the text, you are afforded the opportunity to mention your team name, slogan, group activity or group goals. This builds team interest and is a great retention tool. A group text is just the beginning of group communication. The best way to use group texting is covered in the chapter "Be Mobile."

Once your group grows to 30-50 members, it's time to start formally recognizing your team name. One of the easiest and most inexpensive ways to do this is to create a team t-shirt. Give the first few away for accomplishments, and then everyone on your team will want one. You can also create hats, signs, noise makers— anything you can get your team name or logo on to help create an identity for your group at company events that will make your people proud! Don't be shy about selling these items at team events to help recoup your costs. Your team members will be happy to contribute, because they'll be proud to be part of a successful team.

Once the team name has been established, it's time to promote the culture. Use your overall team success as a challenge to keep people motivated and goal-oriented. Foster competition between your members and other organizations in your company. Make sure to keep the competition healthy and positive to maintain a high level of respect for team leaders throughout the company. Don't hurt the team spirit of the company by putting down other teams, leaders or organizations. And don't create rifts among other leaders in the company or with people in your upline who are not a part of the team atmosphere. Creating team culture also creates a mutual interest of team success among people who are not in the same upline or downline, or might not have a financial interest in the person they are working with, but because they are part of a "team" they want to be able to work together for the benefit of the entire group. So, doing contests or promoting team goals will bring the group together even more. No doubt about it, you are the spoke of the wheel for your business. It's up to you to build confidence, recruit new members, encourage your leaders, foster culture and goodwill, and be the leader of your organization. What you say and do matters. Make no mistake, leaders will look to you for answers and advice every step of the way, so establishing and cultivating a group dynamic is essential to your business.

I often tell people at major events, conventions, trainings or meetings that the time you spend working with your team during intermission or breaks, is in some ways even more valuable than the actual event itself. Getting my team together no matter how big or small for a team dinner or team meeting during a major company event has given me incredible opportunities for leadership development, recognition and great strategy sessions. I recommend piggy backing off of larger company events to orchestrate team events. Conduct special pre-meetings, parties or breakout sessions with your team during event breaks or the day before/after the event takes place. This is easy to do if you plan ahead of time. You have to be able to fit it into the event schedule, so establishing a good game plan with everyone is key. If you are going to do something before the event or after the event, you have to let people know in advance so they can plan their trip accordingly. My best advice is to do something during the event if at all possible. As long as it doesn't take away from anything the company is doing. You don't want your team to skip out on anything just so that they can hang out with you. That will send the exact opposite message of what you are trying to create. You could also do it with another team, if yours is not big enough to warrant an exclusive event. If the company is hosting the event on site, you may be able to find another meeting room at the same location or nearby to make it easy for people to get there. You could charge per head or ask leaders to split the costs with you if there are costs involved. This type of private function will allow you to cast the vision for your team that will motivate them to achieve more as a group. It is also a great opportunity for your leaders to see how you put team events together properly, so when it is their time to run their own events, they are prepared.

Events are also excellent for team recognition, since you will often have people who are very committed to the organization and who are performing well, but who may not be recognized at a large company event. This time may also be used as a platform to edify your top performers in the group, and even give them a moment for some spotlight of their own. Recognition is one of the most important ways of building confidence, highlighting strengths and keeping your team on the same page. It is also a crucial tool for retention because there will be several people who appreciate and look forward to the individual recognition you give to your team. There will be several people inside your organization who play a role in the growth and advancement of the team, but might not ever make it to the upper echelons of your company's achievement levels. It is up to you as the leader of your organization to take the time to recognize people for the different types of contributions that they make to the organization. Not only will this encourage more people to step up and lend a hand in other ways than just making more sales, but you will also keep people focused on helping the team reach its goals regardless of what their personal achievement level may be. I try to recognize people who help with organization, infrastructure, and volunteer at team events because these areas are often overlooked by the standard company recognition.

I try to provide recognition at every event. It is usually not formal with awards or plaques, but is more group recognition in front of the room for doing things that are often overlooked, but are also equally important to events and operations running smoothly for the team. I also try to highlight up-and-coming leaders, so they will see what the spotlight can feel like if they continue to perform at an above average level.

Here are some suggestions for other team activities:

- **Team Night Out:** Often, I will go out after our events with key leaders and volunteers for dinner or a fun activity. Depending on the type of activity you choose, you can make this event for key people or your entire organization. I would involve as many people as possible from your team at least once a month. You can do things like bowling, putt-putt golf, dinner, laser tag, play arcade games or even attend sporting events or concerts.

- **Friday Mixers:** At least once a month we will have a mixer with our entire team in each market that will be an opportunity to hang out. No presentation and *no* mention of the business. We open this event to prospects as well, and it gives us a chance to share our culture and unity with prospective customers or representatives in a very relaxed and comfortable atmosphere. We instruct the members to deflect questions about the business if their prospects ask them about the company or the products, and keep the focus on the fun and bonding time we are all having together. Usually after an event like that you will see a huge spike in attendance at your next presentation because the people who came to the mixer will be looking forward to actually finding out what you do!

- **Family Events:** I also like to put together family events like barbeques and picnics so that our team members can bring their entire family. It is easier for spouses and children to understand the time and energy that their parent may be spending on their business if they can see what our team culture is all about. I have often had team members open up after events like this about how a spouse or family member wasn't supportive of their business before our family event, but after they got a chance to meet everyone and see the friendships and relationships we have created around our business, their outlook completely changed and they became more supportive. Most of these activities can easily involve your team's significant others, but you should always try to plan something easy for them to bring the whole family to at least once a quarter.

- **Team-Building Events:** It's also a good idea to try to put together team-building events with your key leaders and top performers as well. It may be difficult to put an event like this on with your entire organization, but it is very easy to do something like this with your key people. Events that will allow you to bond as a team and create memories through experiences will be the things that can take your whole team to the next level. I have taken key leaders to personal development seminars, group competitions like laser tag, paintball, capture the flag, obstacle courses and other events that encourage group participation and interaction. Try to plan something like this as soon as possible, if you haven't done this type of activity before.

- **Trips:** Trips are where I have made the biggest impact with my top leaders throughout my career. There is just something about bonding with your team in a relaxed and casual environment that creates memories and friendships that will last a lifetime. Most Direct Sales and Network Marketing companies have trip contests and incentives involving travel, but even if your company doesn't offer a way to travel with your team, you should get together with your team and start planning your first team trip now. My suggestion is to do a trip that is family-friendly, especially if the majority of your team has families. The last thing you want to do is plan an awesome team trip that excludes everyone's significant family members. I personally like doing resort-style properties that have everything in one place so that your group can socialize around dinner, the pool or whatever activities are located on the property. If you have to leave the property, then normally the groups get split up and you don't get the same effect.

Although SPENDING time with your team is important, I think you'll agree that MAKING the most of that time is equally, if not more, important. Creating quality time entails getting your group together in a variety of ways that will help build belief, friendships, accountability, motivation, creativity and loyalty. After all, your team is really another extension of your own beliefs and commitments; they are, therefore, aligned to help you build your business, through thick and thin, and ultimately achieve success. If you consider your team as your family, and you offer them your time, guidance, mind and heart, there's no telling how far you can go.

5

There Is an Event for That

*I*f there's one thing I have learned after years in this industry, it's this—people are different, vastly different. Not everyone responds to the same approach. What appeals to one person may not appeal to another. I have noticed the same trend in different markets, different countries and different cities: A variety of people were only attending one type of event. Granted, there may be people in your business who go to the majority of meetings and functions, but they are also in the minority compared with your overall team and organization. Therefore, it is crucial that you promote, schedule and offer various activities in every market, so that you can reach all demographics and personality types. Just like Apple says, "There is an app for that", well in this industry I say, "There is an event for that!"

> **Develop a strategy to draw people to events.**

This realization really hit home when I started a market completely from scratch and had to orchestrate every event myself. Initially, I was at the mercy of people who were willing to show up and bring prospects. As a result, the events were inconsistent and I noticed the same people frequently attended the same types of events. I also noticed that it wasn't the results they were getting from the events that kept them from attending certain events, but, rather, the way those events spoke to their personalities and interests. This insight led me to create specific events to reach certain audiences, demographics and personalities. Not only is it important to have a variety of events for your representatives and distributors, but also for your prospects. Personality types are the same for members as they are for your potential prospects. Initially it was a major time commitment to orchestrate these various events, but eventually this system developed enough leaders that I had a multitude of people to eventually take over the events when I wasn't there.

I hope you will use as many of the events as possible, that I outline in this chapter, in your weekly or monthly strategy. Once I began to use a variety of events regularly in all of my markets, I started to notice a more consistent level of sales production, because it allowed me to produce a variety of results throughout the week rather than relying on individual activity or only *one big event* a week. I have seen teams put all their "eggs" in one basket and as a result their weekly sales success depended on how well that meeting did, and when a holiday or special event popped up that posed a conflict with the once-a-week event, their sales would be devastated that week. By using a variety of events in each of your markets, you eliminate the risk of having a bad week based on the success or failure of one big event.

After-Hours Larger Events

During my time in this industry I have met many people with a 9-to-5 mentality. In other words, once the work day is over, 9-to-5ers believe work should be over, which means they don't like to do *anything* after hours. Not working after the 5 p.m. whistle blows is a way we are conditioned, so it's no surprise that working after 5 p.m. for most people is a foreign concept. Keep this in mind when you see prospects or customers after hours. Most people who are working this type of business are doing so in addition to a full-time job, and so many of them only focus on after-hours events to build their business. If you develop a strategy to draw people to events after hours, consider the level of participation your current team may be able to contribute after hours. Your prospects and your team members may have time conflicts after hours ranging from: children, church, work projects, sports, organizations or other engagements. So, take all of these things into consideration when you start to lay out what your after-hour activities should look like.

Some of what we are about to discuss will carry over into other events, but let this be your foundation for the strategy you use when you set up your events:

1) **Day of the week:** It's important to consider "standing" events that occur on certain days of the week. I try to avoid local sporting events, and church or religious activities whenever possible. I also try to avoid Mondays because it is usually the most stressful work day and can create unforeseen circumstances that could cause people to reschedule for a Monday evening event. I also avoid Fridays because it is a day when people generally plan family activities or like to go out on the town, and there are also local sporting events in some markets on Fridays. I try to stay away from Wednesdays if I can because of church or religious functions. I don't like making people choose between events and their religion. That normally leaves the best days for meetings as Tuesday or Thursday. These tend to be the best days of the week to get the highest percentage of both your team members and your potential prospects to your after-hour events.

2) **Time of the event:** Time is just as important as the day of the week you choose for events. Make sure you don't start too late so people can get back to their families and other responsibilities at a decent hour, and also take into account that they need enough time to get their work day finished and possibly drive through traffic to actually make it to your event. I hold meetings earlier in small markets than I do in larger markets due to the lack of traffic, and the ease of getting to the meeting location. In most markets I start evening events at 7 p.m. or 7:30 p.m. at the latest. Consider the combined amount of time the event will take to make the appropriate decision regarding what time your event should start. I also recommend that your presentations not be more than one hour. Your prospects will appreciate you for respecting their time and other commitments that they

may have after your event. Most of your prospects who do not have a vested interest in your business or products will have a very difficult time maintaining a high level of attention and participation in an event that lasts longer than one hour.

3) **The market or group you are trying to reach:** It's important to plan events to cover the personality dynamics of your prospects and team. This is one of the most common things people overlook when they plan events. They generally stay with the same format at a hotel or meeting facility that is on par with industry standards. But it's not the only way to build your business! Ensure you create events to attract people who also want to have fun and interact socially, which can also draw the traditional business people who would prefer something a little more serious and professional but also like to have a good time. For younger demographics, fun and relaxed parties, mixers and happy hours are much more effective. On the other hand, formal business luncheons are *great* for attracting serious, business-minded professionals. Before you plan your schedule or events, sit down and dissect your team and prospects and make sure the event fits the demographic you are trying to reach. I will explain how to reach these different groups later in the chapter.

4) **Who can participate:** Consider which leaders and key team members within your organization will be able to participate in the actual event. There may be leaders or new people with enormous potential who may have a continuous conflict with the date and time you choose for your after-hours events. One way to avoid this is to get buy-in from every major participant before you actually select the date and time of the event. Let them feel like they are involved in the decision making and empower them by explaining reasons for choosing certain dates and times and then ask them what works best for their market. This will keep them

from making excuses down the road based on time conflicts that may have that existed when you planned the event. If everyone you have on your list agrees with the date and time, you can move forward to the next step.

5) **Who will bring supplies:** Your venue will dictate what you need to bring to run the event. Consider registration requirements, audio/visual (AV) equipment and supplies. Having a registration table with friendly greeters is a must for a larger event to go off smoothly, so guests can see a smiling face when they arrive, which will make them more receptive and relaxed. AV equipment will vary based on the venue, so make sure you solve this issue beforehand so you'll know what to expect. Some venues may have some AV and some will have none at all. So decide how you will present and share your information, if you will need a projector, for instance, or if the venue has TVs or a projector built into the room or venue. I try to find a location that already has flat screen TVs that can connect to a laptop or AV equipment already in the room, if possible. If you are travelling to the event, have someone take care of all of this for you so that all you have to do is show up and make the actual presentation. Make sure you have someone responsible for samples, enrollment forms, product materials, signs or any other materials you need for your event. I try to delegate all of this, if possible. I also make people feel involved when I am delegating. Rather than just calling or texting them to bring something, I ask in team meetings, "Who would like to help out with these items?" If there's a cost involved with supplies, I ensure the volunteer does not have to cover the expense out-of-pocket.

We either all contribute, or we find a way to offset the cost of the meeting by having team members contribute or by charging a small fee to members who attend. I also like to explain to people that this is their business, as much as it is mine; that means they need to invest in their business sometimes, and I remind them that if it were not for the group effort, they would have to orchestrate this entire event by themselves. So, contributing a small amount of time or money to the overall event is a small price to pay versus doing the entire thing yourself. Depending on your company presentation or products, there may be slight variations of this information or of the materials I just described, but just make sure that, if at all possible, you are not doing all of this by yourself. This is a great way to increase some natural leadership by giving other people inside your organization the ability to step up and contribute to the overall group by contributing time, money or supplies.

6) **Who will run the event:** This is one of my primary leadership development tools for my organization. It's important to give up-and-coming producers the ability to hone their speaking skills in front of groups by allowing them to participate and feel responsible for the successful outcome of the event. If you empower people as you delegate responsibilities, it will not only free you up to affect more markets, but it will also give you a path to create leadership skills by having people hold themselves accountable early on in their career. I have seen some leaders who try to do everything themselves, and never empower their people to step up and help contribute. Although, this may be an ego boost and give those leaders more stage time and recognition, the downside of this is that you will have far less leadership development in the long run. If you delegate effectively, however, and allow as many people as possible to participate in the actual running, planning and organizing of the event, your organization will grow faster and depend less on you. This allows people to see what putting an entire event together from start to finish entails. If you do all of this yourself without any help from your team, they will always depend on you to do everything for them and then nothing will get done unless

you are involved in everything. I try to allow people to watch me go through the steps when I put events together, and then I slowly start delegating in a way that allows them to take on some responsibility, but I try not to set up the event so that the entire event hinges on one person. This will keep you from having any unexpected "ball drops," that can sometimes happen when new leaders get overwhelmed with too much responsibility, and the whole event is dependent on one person. Just walk through your event from start to finish like we are doing here, and try to have someone help with each aspect, at a minimum, and ideally have a group of people rotate responsibilities.

7) **The format of the event:** The format of your event will vary depending on your product or service. However, I am going to lay out a basic meeting flow along with reasoning behind each aspect so you not only have an outline, but also understand why each step has equal responsibility in the overall successful outcome of the event.

   a. **Introduction and Welcome:** This is your opportunity to connect with the audience and also edify the speaker. The introduction can be a great way to break the ice and create a relaxed environment. Tell a joke or have some fun with the crowd before the main speaker comes to deliver the message. Edification of the speaker is *crucial*! If you provide the *best* introduction possible, it establishes them as an expert, and also keeps them from having to list their accomplishments. I have always said that if there is a good introduction and the speaker can carry themselves well, then there's no reason for them to recount their achievements because the audience is already familiar with what they have done.

   b. **Message:** I believe in promoting the message above the messenger. I have seen people who were not considered great presenters sign up the majority of the room, and I have seen great presenters not sign up anyone in the room. Your company should have some type of presentation or message for representatives to share with potential prospects and customers. Since the message should be fairly uniform, this is your chance to do some more leadership development. In a perfect world you should always try to have your most accomplished leader share the message along with a new person. This will present two different styles and two different points of view. Many times when I speak at events, I will have someone whom I am trying to groom into being a better speaker share the presentation with me. So, it's not necessarily about the speaker being perfect as it is about the message. If you are going to split up the presentation, select easier sections for the new person to relieve some of the pressure. Also, make sure everyone is on the same page with what information is being shared, and by whom, and try to work with everyone on their sections before the actual event. If you have time, let them practice in front of you or a small group first, just to get some of the jitters out of the way. Following this method will give you a fresh supply of presenters in every market, and it will also create more leaders inside your organization.

c. **Testimonials:** This can be the most powerful part of the actual event, if it's done properly, due in part to the old saying: "Facts tell, and stories sell." This is your chance to share all of the hot stories you have in each market; however, the person sharing their story at a live event should be properly coached before they share a testimonial. A good testimony should have a few key elements:

i. **Short background:** When presenters share their background and current occupation, it allows people with similar backgrounds or stories to relate to their story. This should be the shortest part of the testimonial. It shouldn't be their life story, but just simple information that will allow the audience to know who the speaker actually is. Also, ensure that they don't share any unnecessary information about who initially shared the opportunity with them, what they thought at the beginning, or what happened during their first week. Doing so, runs the risk of people thinking: "Who cares?" Rather, keep it precise and to the point by saying something like: "My name is Frank and I am from Dallas, Texas, and I have been a high school football coach for 11 years."

ii. **What life was like before:** This is where the person giving the testimonial will explain what their life was like before they were introduced to the business opportunity or product. This will vary depending on your product or service, but the main point here is to show a "before" so that you can share a powerful "after" with the next element of the testimonial. This can be anything from lifestyle, wellness, type of house, type of car or anything that has been improved either because of the business opportunity or because of your product.

iii. **What life is like now:** This is the presenter's chance to share the success they have had since being introduced to the products or the business opportunity. I try to split the testimonials—half business success stories and half product success stories. This will give a good mix of stories to appeal to potential customers, business prospects and people who may be interested in both. If all you do is have people talk about the business, people will tend to forget about the products and their impact; likewise, if you have too many people talk about the products, you will encourage people to be customers without cultivating their interest to become distributors. People sharing their testimonials should just share the high points of what has happened to them based on the topic they are covering with their testimonial. The business testimony should focus on: results, growth, amount of time, change in lifestyle or living situation, financial benefits, lifestyle benefits, time freedom, etc. The product testimony should focus on: results, effects, usage stories, savings, value, experience, service, etc.

A good rule of thumb is that each testimonial should be between 30-60 seconds, depending on the amount of testimonials you have at the event. If you have more than five, I would keep each testimonial to 30 seconds; and if you have less than five, they could each be 60 seconds. Some companies may have specific rules pertaining to stories or testimonials at public events due to regulations surrounding nutritional and wellness products, so please make sure you check with your company and include any disclaimers you need to be compliant with company policies and procedures.

d. **Call-to-action:** Don't miss the opportunity to get a decision from everyone in the room at one time. The call-to-action should have a few elements to help people get to a point where they can make a comfortable decision on the spot. Ask people to make a choice from options rather than a simple "yes" or "no." I usually provide perspective by telling the audience that I was sitting right where they are when I first was introduced to the opportunity, and I stress that the only difference between them and me is that I saw it before they did. Once I go through the particular close or wrap up of the presentation or company materials, I re-explain their options. This way there is no confusion between the business, the product and the price points. I also let them know that their decision is time sensitive because every day that goes by we are going to be talking to more people and eventually we will be talking to more of their friends and family, and they will continue to hear about the success stories involving the product from more people around them, so instead of waiting for that to happen, they should get started tonight and be the one who is doing the "telling" rather than the person who is doing the "listening." Fear of loss is one of the most powerful emotions to elicit an immediate response, so if you can incorporate some of this into your presentation you should see an increase in your on-the-spot enrollments.

e. **Announcements:** After you allow everyone in the room to sign up, introduce the market leader, who will make any important announcements about upcoming events or training. This allows new enrollees to get off to a fast start by knowing when they can bring potential prospects or customers to the next event. This is also a good time to schedule all of your new enrollments for a game-planning session, which we touched on in a previous chapter.

8) **Where to hold the event:** Now that we have covered the logistics around how to run after-hours events, let's look at a few details on where to have the events along with location benefits.

    a. **Hotel Events:** Hotel meetings are a traditional approach to after-hours public events. I've been running these events for more than a decade, and I like them for several reasons: they can accommodate very large groups; they have ample parking; they are usually in good locations; they usually have AV equipment; and they have a professional atmosphere. There are other benefits to hotel meetings, but there are also disadvantages, such as: you have to pay for the room; the dates are sometimes not flexible; the AV equipment may be an additional charge; you have to plan farther in advance; and sometimes you must pay in advance. Once your group gets very large, a hotel and public meeting space will be your only option to host an after-hours event. However, that's a *positive problem*! Another thing I noticed is that sometimes people tend to have guests not show up to hotel meetings because they know it is a "meeting." Whether it's because they've already spent all day at work in meetings or whether they have a pre-conceived notion about what they're coming to the hotel for, getting objections to the public meeting is something your new people will have to contend with more frequently than they will when it is held at a private residence or restaurant.

    b. **Social Public Events/Happy Hours:** Lately I have been holding more events at public places like bars, restaurants and lounges. Here is my theory on this:

people are used to going out with their friends and family to have food or drinks at local bars and restaurants. However, they may not be used to going to hotel meetings or public meetings with their friends and family. So, if I can keep it more like a traditional invitation from a friend to have food or drinks and meet some other people, then I usually get a higher percentage of people to show up for the event. This does not mean that you should mislead anyone about the purpose of the event. It just seems to be much more comfortable to get friends to sit down at a bar or restaurant and hear about something that their friend or family member has gotten excited about. This may not work with every single product and service out there, but I am confident that it will work with most of them. It has been the primary driver for the growth of my team over the last couple of years. We usually try to find a restaurant that has a private room or banquet area to reserve just for the hour of the actual event itself. This keeps the space available for the restaurant to use for other patrons which helps eliminate rental cost, and allows people to mix and mingle freely at the bar area if they have one.

We generally have everyone arrive about 30 minutes early for a mix and mingle, and to linger around the bar area if there is one, and if not, try to keep people flowing freely in the banquet room rather than sitting at tables and not interacting. Also, make sure you start on time so that people who got there early do not get anxious. If you promote it properly, you should have the majority of people there early for the mix and mingle, allowing you to start on time very easily. I have also held these meetings a little earlier than normal in some markets to fit with more of a "Happy Hour" atmosphere, where people can easily bring co-workers after they leave the office. If I am doing a "Happy Hour" event, I keep them in a comfortable atmosphere and try to do a shortened, more relaxed presentation that keeps people very casual and comfortable. This concept is more effective if you can reserve the bar entirely or if they have a private room you can use for the actual presentation.

9) **Grand Openings:** Although your company may not promote its products or services through house parties traditionally, you can successfully launch people to a fast start with their business using the party concept. A "house party" is really just a term used to describe a member who gets their friends to come to their home so they can share their products, services or opportunity with them. I prefer to call these events "Grand Openings" instead of "parties." No one opens a retail business without having some type of ribbon cutting or grand opening. This is your chance to have everyone in your organization expose the best people in their warm market as fast as possible. The biggest reason to do this is because it's easier to get someone to your house than it is to get them to a hotel or public meeting. Why? Because once again we can have a new person do something natural that they've done before. They may not have invited someone to a hotel or public meeting, but everyone has invited their friends or family over to their home. Why try to reinvent the wheel by having them do something that they have never done before? Instead, have them invite 20 of their closest friends and family over to their home for a grand opening and get them off to a *great* start! Here are my tips to having a great "Grand Opening":

   a. **Set Expectations:** For a successful invitation, set the proper expectations. Most people assume if they invite five people, then five people will show up, but that's usually not the case. Sometimes circumstances will arise that will keep people from attending their event. This happens to everyone, and it is not because they don't want to go or they don't want to support them; it's just because life happens. So, to have a successful event, they should invite three to four times the number of people they want to actually have at their event. So if they want to have 20 people there, they need to invite at least 60 people to the event. This may discourage some people, but if you explain why this happens and set the tone from the beginning, they will not be devastated when they invite five and only one person shows up.

b. **Teach the Invite:** This is the easiest way for new people to invite prospects to see their business or products because they've already asked people to come over to their home before. All they have to do is keep it simple and similar to what they would do if they were inviting someone over to watch a football game or hang out.

NOTE: They do not need to tell their friends that they are having a "Grand Opening." The only person who knows this is a grand opening is the member doing the inviting. We only use this term to describe the actions of what we are trying to accomplish so that the concept makes sense to a new person.

The invite is very simple -- just two steps:

1. Are you free tomorrow night at 7:30?

2. **If yes:** "Come over to my house, I have something I want you to see."

   If no: "It's OK, we'll catch up later."

This makes it simple and also keeps people from asking a lot of questions. If they do ask questions, say the following: "It's very important to me and I need you to be here."

c. **Last-Minute Invite:** One of the excuses I hear from new representatives when I am teaching them how to invite to a "Grand Opening" is that they need to give their guests *notice*. That is actually the furthest thing from the truth. We live in a last-minute society driven by current events that get the most attention. Most people do not make plans more than a week out for social occasions. There are things that get put on the calendar because they happen at a specific time for a specific reason, but most social experiences with friends and family other than major holidays, birthday parties and the Super Bowl can happen just about any day at any time. Try to think about it like going for a drink during happy hour with a group of friends after work. Or, think of your last trip to dinner or the movies with a friend. Did you plan those two weeks in advance?

Most social engagements get planned the same day and sometimes literally an hour or so before the event. Most movies and happy hours that I have been to have been planned like this: a friend calls me and says *"Hey, I just got off work and I am headed to happy hour, want to join me?"* This is the same way I normally ask my friends to dinner and the movies, as well. And this is the same way you can invite for "Grand Openings" or really any type of event for that matter. The reason why this invite is so powerful in the social world is because it is easy and simple. If someone asked me to go to happy hour like I just described and I didn't have any plans I would simply say, "Yes, where are we meeting?" If the person is free then they generally accept the invitation, and there are not a lot of things that can happen to derail the plans from the time the call is made until the person shows up. If you invite someone a week in advance, there are too many unknown factors out there that can keep them from attending whatever event you have asked them to attend.

These unknown variables include a sick child, a fight with a co-worker, an unplanned event, a long day at the office or something that comes up with a window of 24-48 hours before your event. These are the reasons why people don't show up to something they have previously committed to attend. The only way you can eliminate circumstances that keep your guests from attending is to wait as long as possible to invite them. **The smaller the window of time, the more likely they are to show up at your event.** This is the reason I teach new people to only invite 24-48 hours before the event *maximum*. The best invites, in my opinion, are the ones that happen the night before or the same day. You may have some people who already have commitments, but the ones who don't will have a *very high* likelihood of showing up to your event because you have narrowed the window of distractions that can keep them from attending.

d. **Follow Up:** Once you set the expectations on how many people to invite and how to invite them, it's important to follow up with them to check on their progress. Many people leave this step out, which is unfortunate, because it can cause the most damage to your new member and your team. If you've already committed your time to coordinating a "Grand Opening" with one of your new members, then it's equally as important to set aside the time to follow up on their progress. I require anyone whom I am assisting with a "Grand Opening" to give me an RSVP list with names and phone numbers the night before the event. If we have scheduled the event last minute then I will just make the invite calls with them so that I know they will have a successful event. However, if it is planned a few days in advance, like the majority of events are, I will get that list from them the night before and walk through it with them and ask them about all of the guests, and try to feel out what the crowd will be like for the event. This allows you to follow up without having to wonder if they really made the calls. As I go through the list and ask them to tell me a little about each person, I will be able to tell how committed everyone is, and whether or not they have invited enough people to have a successful event.

e. **Have Entire Team Provide Support:** A "Grand Opening" is not just for the people who are hosting the event; it is also a chance for the rest of your organization to support the new person and get some guests there for themselves. It adds to the energy of the event if you have current customers or members at the Grand Opening, and they can also share their testimonials at the end of the presentation. These extra people will help fill the room, and make the new person feel more comfortable by taking some pressure off filling the entire house by themselves.

The flow of the event should go the same as for the public meeting, but you may not have as many testimonials to share, so you could always have a few people on standby with their phones, and after you're done with the information, you can put some members or customers on speaker phone to share their stories. It is also not necessary to have a top leader or speaker do your "Grand Opening" presentation for you. You can very easily use a web presentation, pre-recorded webinar, DVD or even a recorded conference call to share information with people in lieu of a live presentation. Remember, the prospective members or customers have never seen the information before, so they don't know what is normal. Also, don't make a big production out of food, drinks or entertainment. Of course, some people will go all out; but remember, we're striving for duplication and if people see that all the host had to do was invite people over and they made money just for inviting, then everyone will want to have their own "Grand Opening" as soon as possible. If their prospects think they have to prepare a bunch of food or have a catered event, it will discourage them from having their own "Grand Opening". If you need anything for your "Grand Opening", have guests or other members bring items so that the host only has to focus on inviting.

10) **Business Luncheons:** If you want to attract professional people to your products and business who usually have the most influence, I recommend putting on at least one business luncheon in your markets every week. The meeting format will be the same, with a few minor changes that can give you an added level of success.

   a. **Have a Set Menu:** Arrange a set menu with the restaurant before your event with only three items to choose from so you can have people select their choice as soon as they walk in. I usually have menus printed on paper so all my guests have to do is circle their selection and hand it to the wait staff. I've also used colored cards or poker chips to designate the item they've selected by placing the color card or chip in front of them at the table so that the wait staff doesn't have to interrupt the event when they bring in the food. I explain the system to the restaurant in advance and let them know once we start our event, *no one* should be talking or making noise; they need to just bring in the food and set it down in front of the guests as quietly as possible. I also try to do a set price for the lunch, fountain drink, tax and tip, so people can have the appropriate amount ready when we conclude the event. Make sure this is done beforehand to ensure your luncheon goes off without a hitch, and that people can plan for what the cost will be for themselves and their guests if they are paying for them.

b. **Shorten Your Presentation:** I always make it a point to tell people to arrive at noon and then we'll start no later than 12:15 p.m., which gives us enough time to do a 30-minute presentation and then about five to 10 minutes to wrap up and sign people up on the spot. Don't make the business presentation too long, or you will have people leave during your presentation because they have to get back to work. Also, make sure you leave time for people to pay their bill and fill out sign-up forms or product order forms. You will create major follow-up obstacles for your team afterwards if your lunch events run late.

c. **Teach People to Invest in Their Business:** When it comes to inviting prospects for a business luncheon, I teach people to invest in their business. If you do a good job negotiating with the restaurant, your business luncheons should be around $10 per person for lunch, drink, tax and tip. This way someone can invite friends or co-workers to lunch and just say "Can I buy your lunch, I have something I want to show you?" This is a no-brainer. People never turn down a free meal, and if you run your events properly and get sales, then your team will know it makes sense to keep inviting and paying for lunch because they are gaining more customers.

11) **Negotiating Rooms for Events:** If you take your time negotiating, you can find a great spot for your event, and

create a great business relationship with the business owner where you host your events. Here are my key negotiating points for your event:

a. **Be Flexible:** If you want the best deal for your group, be flexible about the date and time of your event. I will often ask the restaurant owner or manager, "What is your slowest lunch day?" After they answer, if that day of the week works for me I will try to schedule our event for that day so that it is a win/win for us and the local business. This same tactic works for hotel meeting rooms. I just find out what day of the week they have the least amount of bookings for their meeting spaces. As long as the dates and times that are readily available do *not* conflict with what we have already discussed in this chapter involving the appropriate time and days of the week, I would try to make one of these "off" days work for your event.

b. **Book in Advance:** Let the manager or owner know that you want to do this for several consecutive weeks, and that it will be a small group at first, but it will get bigger over time. Go ahead and lock in your date and time now along with your rate, so that as your group gets bigger the owner doesn't try to raise the rates on you. This allows your team to know in advance that this is the day and location of your regular business luncheon. Also, explain to the business owner that this is a win/win because the people you invite would not normally be coming into this establishment on this specific day and time. These people are coming to this business because you are promoting it to people in your local community. This will also give them future business, because your members are loyal, and since you have chosen this location they will also be loyal to this business in the future. I also explain that since you are hosting these events regularly, they should look at these events like "free advertising," because you are out there promoting these events at this specific location to all of your members and prospects on websites, emails, texts and personal invitations. That is *major* advertising for their brand and business, and they would normally pay a lot of money for this type of exposure.

c. **Find Other Ways to Make it a Win/Win:** Here are some other ways to make it a win/win for the business by asking questions like:

- "What are your food items that have the best margin that we could use for our luncheon?"

- "Is there a meeting room that has an odd shape or configuration that you don't normally book as often?"

- "Is there a night of the week you want to attract more business?"

- "Is there a new dish you want to try out or get some feedback on?"

Remember to treat these business owners professionally, and don't just think about what you want and what's in it for you. If you have a **great attitude** when you negotiate, you will usually create a **great relationship** that will probably earn you a lot of perks and benefits personally from that particular establishment. My hope is that this chapter has given you an in-depth look at different meetings and events to use to take your business to new heights. I have found this aspect of the business is constantly evolving as I find more creative ways to reach different demographics and personality types around the world.

6

Event-to-Event Management

*I*n this chapter we'll cover one of the most valuable points in this entire book: mastering event- to-event management. This has been one of the secret weapons of my career, and is a concept that is incredibly valuable whether you are managing a small group or a team of thousands. Getting people to events is what provides credibility and belief in your product, builds leadership, and instills confidence in your team. It also provides yet another opportunity to solidify culture among your team, which cannot be created without event attendance.

In every organization I have been part of, I have consistently produced and run the largest local events, which effectively draw the biggest numbers to national and international meetings. If you don't master the skill of event-to-event management, you will likely have lower retention rates because people in this business have a tendency to quit when they don't create a bond with the team or a connection to the company. You will also not fulfill your team's true potential for growth if you don't get them to events, resulting in a lack of motivation and excitement. How you manage the calendar leading up to and coming out of events is also critical to maximizing the time and energy spent getting members to these events.

Most leaders experience two separate problems with event management:

1. The inability to get enough people to attend
2. Failing to leverage productivity going into or (the bigger problem) coming out of events

The first problem is solved by proper promotion. Most people think that just telling someone about the next event is enough to get them there. Whether it's a small regional event or a major national or international company get-together, you must become a master promoter

Make company events your first priority!

to get your team to participate. And promotion begins and ends with preparation. Planning ahead allows you to maximize the work you put in before the event and the results coming out of it. It's crucial that you make company events your first priority. Conventions, rallies and conferences at the national and international level are the most important opportunities for your organization to unite, fostering confidence and commitment among your team. Getting your team to these types of events will open their eyes to all of the possibilities that your company, products and ideas can provide for their future. So when you're planning your calendar, make company events a top priority and don't plan anything that could conflict with your team's attendance.

As a leader you should attend every major event to set the example for the rest of your organization. No one remembers if you've been to every event in the past; what they will remember is whether you are or *are not* at the current event. Not making events a priority can lead to resentment by your team and lack of credibility in your leadership. So once you layout your calendar with major events, your next task is to review your schedule for any local events or trainings that are important for all of your markets. If you work with teams in multiple markets, create a calendar for each market to help you plan better and stay on top of the current event promotion. Remember not to plan any team meetings or presentations that directly conflict with events that the company, other reps, or other teams may be running. You don't want to create a situation where people have to pick and choose which events to go to, and there are plenty of days and times to allow for all types of events. You also don't want to set a bad example for your team or other reps by organizing a competing event that may create the reputation that you are not a "team" player; which also means not scheduling meetings too close to other major events that could force members of your team to choose which one to attend.

Proper promotion begins with employing a single-minded focus. If you want people to attend, make it the only thing they think about or at least the "most important" thing on their minds. A problem arises when you provide your team with multiple events to promote and plan for, because it gives them the ability to pick and choose what they "think" is the most important thing to focus on. Often, with new team members, what they *think* is important is not always the *most important*.

Once you have international, national and local events on your calendar, add your team meetings, presentations and anything else that fits with your business and schedule. Once your calendar is set, you can get into event-to-event management. I focus on the upcoming six-to-eight weeks of events as I go through my plan for proper promotion. I then look for opportunities that I can create to drive sales and boost energy within my organization surrounding upcoming events. Some of the things I look for are:

1. Who can be recognized at upcoming events for achieving certain levels, ranks or promotions?
2. Are there any company promotions, contests or incentives that can be used?
3. Is there a chance for contests or incentives I can create to boost performance before events?
4. What is the *next* event we are promoting?
5. What is next *major* event that should be on the calendar?

It helps to put these items on a promotion list. Keep that list handy as you go through calls, meetings, one-on-ones, presentations, webinars, emails, texts or any form of contact you have with your organization. There should be a constant plan of attack for your promotion as you interact with your team each day. It should be systematic, and members of your team will start to learn from you and make this the way they communicate with their teams as well.

Here's an example of how to use this list on an individual call:

> "Sally, I wanted to reach out to you and talk about something important. Do you have a minute? Great! I'm excited that you are so close to your next promotion! Did you know all you need is _____ to get recognized for your next rank at the upcoming National Event? I am so proud of you for working so hard. Is there anything I can do to help you hit the promotion before the event? If you put in the sales necessary to hit the promotion, you are also going to be very close to winning the company contest for the month that was just announced! That gives you *two* reasons to work harder over the next three weeks! Also, I wanted to see how your team was preparing for our local training this weekend. This weekend's event will be a great opportunity to get people registered for the National Event, and you should make sure all of your key people are already registered before the training event so they can share testimonials about how excited they are about the National Event so you can get the rest of the group signed up during your training!"

This call walks through four of the five components of proper promotion and is a great example of a call you can have with an up-and-coming leader.

Now, here's an example of using the promotion list on team communication. You could send the following short text to your team that could easily be converted into email format with more information:

> "There are only 16 days left to qualify for our team contest before the National Event, and the opportunity presentation tomorrow night at _____ will be a perfect place to get one step closer to your next promotion!"

This is short and to the point, and highlights four of the five components of proper promotion. I would also follow this up with texts to leaders or key people who may be close to a promotion or rank advancement leading up to the event. This text or email can be sent to a group of people in a specific market or to a specific team that covers the members you are targeting.

An example of this would be:

> "I wanted to give some last-minute information to you that is very time sensitive! We have several people who are just a few sales away from being recognized for new ranks at the National Event next month! I wanted to make sure everyone was aware of these people _____ and recognize them for their hard work. Let's make sure we do everything we can to get these people to their promotions before the event! There are only 16 days left to qualify for the team contest leading up to the National Event, and many people are putting together extra meetings and events so they can create some extra activity to hit the contest! Don't forget, the price of airfare will be going up in 48 hours for the 14-day advance purchase, so book your flights and hotel rooms for the National Event before it's too late!"

In this example I would also include event specifics like location, date, time and the venue at every opportunity to get people even more excited about being there. I try to be very clear and paint pictures of what it will be like, so they can see themselves at the event. These examples did not contain this type of specific information because it will vary for each of you, but try to mention anything you can to create buzz and excitement while at the same time giving them specific information and deadlines.

The larger your team gets, the more important event management becomes. When you successfully promote your events and get your organization to follow suit, it creates a system of duplication resulting in the best attendance possible at every event and the most productivity from your team before and after.

This also allows you to manage your team more effectively, become more mobile and have more free time. Being mobile was one of my motivators for mastering event-to-event management. I wanted to create a system where I was not needed, and when I was away, nobody would notice. I know leaders who have to be in control of everything, and if they aren't, they feel a lack of significance. I'm on the other end of the spectrum. I want to be irrelevant to my team's success. This is the beauty of network marketing, and is one of the reasons I am in this industry. If I wanted to do everything myself, I would pursue another career path. Creating a successful system that can be followed isn't just about creating duplication in sales; it also is very much a result of organization and proper promotion. Leaders who can master this skill will have the best results, and it will appear that they are always working and put in the most time, when in reality they are just good at promoting the "perception" that they are making things happen. To be honest, the more my team grows, the less I work. Why? Because I manage my event-to-event management properly, and it allows me to step back and watch the duplication in my organization.

Getting people to conferences or trainings is only half of the goal; the other half is what happens before and after events. Activities before are usually easier for people to orchestrate, especially if you are a decent promoter. The problem lies in what happens after events to most teams that are not properly prepared. This is what I call an "event hangover." Your calendar must cover a game plan for what happens leading up to the event, and more importantly what happens after. Many who are new to the business tend to focus completely on getting people to the event and proper promotion of the event, while forgetting about the days coming out of that event. So, if you have built your promotion list and you understand what we have discussed so far in the first part of this chapter, you are ready for what I think is even more critical in achieving massive results.

Let's start with what happens leading up to an event. A major event gives you an opportunity to drive your organization to a higher level, especially members motivated by rank and recognition. Members who work harder for achievement, promotion, rank or contests, offer a good opportunity for you to build a game plan and get more work from these people who are motivated by these elements surrounding events. Not only does it allow you to leverage their ambition, it also gives you something to use to lock them into the actual event itself. They're not going to put in all that work and then *not go*! So you have essentially committed them to the actual event and, at the same time, stretched their normal capacity to correspond to the goals which they have set for this event.

The best way to do this is to do an overview of your organization when you lay out your calendar for the next promotion period. Look for people who have potential but who may be underachieving, and look for people who may be close to their next rank or achievement. Once you find out who these key people are, schedule a call with them to get them geared up for this promotion period. Make sure you cover the following on that call:

- What they need to do to hit their next level
- Who on their team can help contribute to their progress or promotion
- What their schedule needs to look like
- The list of the people from their team they need to target to get to the actual event

The last bullet point may seem obvious, but it is often overlooked, and is what can boost your attendance more than anything else to events. Explain to your key players what will happen if they get "their" people to the event and how important that will be in helping them reach their individual goal. Let them help you create an environment of expectation. Create excitement among your team by telling them who will be at the event, what it will be like to connect with and learn from top leaders, how much they will learn and how much fun they will have. This creates a situation where you have "mini promoters" doing the work alongside you as they are constantly reminding people to get registered for the event and make it a priority. Once someone is registered for an event, it changes their psychology, and creates confidence because they are committed. In other words, just the act of helping someone sign up for an event instills belief in themselves, confidence in what they're promoting and a commitment to the organization. By doing so, you are taking them in a direction that can have a lasting effect on their business and their life. At the very minimum, you are showing them what it is like to be part of a team and organization. As a result of their commitment to attend an event, they put in extra effort to help the cause leading up to the actual event itself, allowing more people to be affected in a positive way.

Remember, you're running an organization. Prior to the event, you should also help your team visualize their goals and break them down into the smallest denominators. The easiest way to do this is to work backwards. Find out what their ultimate goal is, and then break it down over the time period leading up to the event. So, I will start with small numbers based on what they can do on a daily basis right now with their current team. I will normally increase their sales numbers gradually over the contest period to account for the growth of their team that is taking place. Then I will make sure the numbers we have put down on the calendar will get them to their ultimate goal during the contest period. I then try to show them the type of work they will have to do in the days ahead to produce the actual results we put on the calendar, taking into consideration, of course, the company's normal averages for the amount of work that it takes to produce customers or sales volume. Once you have the numbers broken down, make sure they understand the task at hand and that they are able to commit that amount of time leading up the event.

You can't just tell your key team members what they need to do to achieve their goal and then expect them to do it! You have to get their total buy-in, and make sure they can commit the time and energy that is necessary for the plan you have laid out for them. Often, I will sign up the team member for the event during this meeting, if they aren't already signed up, or at least get their verbal commitment that they will be there and find out their necessary family arrangements, travel arrangements or other details that have to be taken care of in order for them to be at the actual event. It's a no-brainer, I know, but you'd be surprised how many people have bailed on events last-minute because they waited to buy a flight and then the prices changed. One of the things I do to really make sure someone is committed without sounding like a parent is to ask them "What flight are you coming in on?" This will give you a good indication of how "committed" they really are. Flights are much harder to change than hotels, so this is the best question to key in on if travel is necessary for them to attend the event.

Once you have your key players aligned for the upcoming event, it is time to handle the rest of the organization. This will of course involve your promotion list along with strategies to maximize the actual calendar for the most activity leading up to the event. Plan to offer more meetings or local events in order to maximize the results leading up to the next major event. One thing I like to do is to plan a training that will give me an opportunity to get more signups for the major event before it gets too late. Based on the windows in my calendar, I plan a mini-training, webinar, Saturday training or team get-together that will allow me to train and *more importantly* promote and sign people up for the next major event. So if we are doing a regularly scheduled training and I involve up-and-coming leaders, I make sure everyone is prepped to discuss the next major event during their message. For instance, someone may be talking about value or benefits of the products and I encourage them to weave in a story about how when they went to a major event like the one that is coming up and they saw the other top performers, speakers, owners and executives, it allowed them understand what the products were all about and to really comprehend *just how good they are*. I do the same thing with every topic during the training. I find a way for team leaders to work in stories about the event and I prep them on these key stories before they speak. Then, over the course of the event, I have members share stories about the success they have had because of attending these major events and what role the event has played in the growth of their team.

So by the end of the day, we have accomplished three things all at the same time: *people have gotten trained, we have created action and activity, and several people signed up for the major event.* The biggest thing that will add to your success leading up to these major events is to just look at the calendar and figure out ways you can work in more promotion and more excitement about the upcoming event. This part is easy for most people because the overall concept of getting people to these major events makes a lot of sense and everyone naturally gets excited about it, but the teams who get the best results from the events are the ones who plan properly and maximize the activity leading up to the event itself.

Event Hangover

Now let's look at what happens *after* the event, which is the real problem for most people. "Event hangover" is the silent killer for most teams, companies and organizations. Everyone's so focused on the major event that they forget about the days following the event. Most people in this industry are doing this part time, and they have already taken time and energy away from their family, friends, spouse and job due to the extra work and commitment leading up to the event, then after the event, they feel like they need to "recover." Most people come home and throw their event notes on their desk or on a shelf and "catch up" on whatever they were missing for the last few days or few weeks while they spent time on their "part time" business. This is the *exact opposite result* of what a major event is intended to create.

Companies obviously want to get results leading up to the event, but the purpose of running a good event is to get results afterwards. This is why most companies will try to advance their momentum by having a contest or promotion coming out of major events. However, a problem occurs if the contest is not a real game changer and is not focused on the first 48 hours after the major event, which also contributes to the "hangover effect." The best way to avoid this is to have a calendar of activities that are scheduled to take place after the event. You can lightly promote these activities before the event and then while you are at the event they need to be heavily promoted! If organization is not your strong suit, find someone and work with them to help put a strong calendar of events together focusing on the 48 hours immediately following the event. I target all of my markets and all of my teams in the days and weeks leading up to the major event with extra activities, and I try to prepare them for any announcements or contests that might be unveiled at the major event. During these activities I talk to my key team members and set up a *post-event* plan of attack, and I make sure that everyone understands that when they get home the "real work" begins. I also get them excited about being able to take advantage of new announcements and contests that other teams may not capitalize on due to lack of preparation following the event.

I try to involve as many people as I can in these post event activities that I put together so that more people are focused on working when they get home. If your key team members are committed to helping run these post event activities in advance, the thought of taking some "time off" after the main event won't even cross their minds.

Your main objective should be to make sure everyone has an individual game plan for the "Key 48," which is the first 48 hours following a major event. If you can create activities in this window of time, you will substantially build on the company momentum and multiply your success. I always host a team update call after the National Event to get everyone who was at the event and everyone who was unable to attend on the phone together to recap announcements and talk about the plan of attack for the week. For example, I usually get people who were at the event to share testimonials about their experience so that those who didn't attend can receive some of their energy. I also make sure to promote any contests or company incentives on the call, and I give the 48 Hour game plan to the entire group. If there is not a contest coming out of the event that the company is promoting, then I would suggest putting something together with your key leaders or talking to your upline about making sure there is a contest or group focus coming out of the major event. Why? Because it motivates your organization to build the business using competition and incentive to create extra effort.

Word of advice: If you make a contest for your team, make sure it only lasts a few days so that it forces people to act quickly and not take time off after the event.

Apply the "Key 48" to local events and meetings, as well. For instance, if you have a Saturday training have a "Key 48" plan for the 48 hours following the training, so that they can maximize the information that they just received. If this becomes part of your culture in your organization, you will notice that your team will begin to make all of these preparations without you. Your team will remember the results that they got following the event, *which will also drive attendance* to the next major event. They will also remember that they need to not only focus on the activity before, but the activity following the event as well.

After the event your team will be wearing "company armor," which is what I call it when they are "extra" inspired by everything they just experienced. This "armor" will help them overcome many more normal objections or issues in the days following the event, but if your team takes time off after the event, by the time they get to work, the "armor" will have worn off in most cases. If you don't drive results immediately following the event, you'll not only experience a lapse in energy and motivation, but you'll also witness a lax attitude toward the next event.

In fact, the worst thing that can happen to a team or organization is to properly promote a major event and then not plan for activities following the event. The result is that you get everyone from your team to the event, but they have the worst sales week they've had in months the following week because there was no activity immediately after the event that produced results and rewarded them for attending. So, ensure your team is properly prepared for activity following the event. Otherwise, leaders will attribute their drop in sales to people attending the event, and they will come to the conclusion that the sales dip was a result of people focusing their energy on attending the event rather than working with prospects or customers. When this happens, you have a group that is *very unmotivated* to attend the next major event. So you must capitalize on the momentum and the energy coming out of any event, especially the major ones. You want to create a team that will literally want to walk through walls and do whatever it takes to get to their next rank or receive their next promotion in front of their team at the major events.

You want to create a group that's motivated to not only help themselves by increasing activity in their own business, but that will also help other members of their organization reach their goals as well. That means having game-planning sessions with your team during the event over lunch, dinner or on breaks. I always ask my team things like, "What did you like most about the event?" and "What are you planning to do when you get home?" and "What's your game plan?" These questions will help get your team focused to take action as soon as they get home.

As soon as a major event is over, I will fly out to three or four different cities that week because I don't want the event hangover. I always have these events planned and promoted even before the big event. I want to capitalize on all the time, money and energy my team has put into planning before and after the event. I want my team to have immediate results, because if they get immediate results, they will never miss a major event. And if they continue attending major events, and produce results after each event, then my organization will continue to drive attendance to anything we promote as a team.

Remember, you're running an organization. Look at it from a retail store owner's perspective. Black Friday is one of the biggest business days of the year, and any retail business owner will offer deals and promotions and create extra marketing to leverage the sales holiday; but it doesn't shut its doors after Black Friday is over. The shop moves on to the next promotion that is targeted for the upcoming season, holiday or cultural celebration—in other words, the next big thing. Follow the example of the retail store owner and remember, maintaining your business is about maintaining momentum. That's the difference between treating your organization like a hobby and treating it like a full-fledged business—one that deserves your attention, your planning, your commitment, and your involvement, no matter the time of day, or season.

You have to plan ahead, no matter what. Everyone should know what they're doing before and after events. If you step back and run your business like a business, you won't regret the time and effort you put into it. **Run your business like a CEO, instead of just going through the motions, and you will see results.**

7

Be Mobile

*F*or years, network marketing companies have promoted the dream of "beach money," residual income generated from work that continues to accrue, padding your bank account while you're relaxing on the beach. In fact, that was the "carrot" that attracted me to this industry. That I could work and continue to see the benefits of my efforts, even while on vacation, was, and still remains to be, such a remarkable concept, I was immediately hooked. That's the power of the network—a team always accomplishes more than the individual. I realized at an early age that one person can only do so much, producing income based on his or her efforts alone. But when you have a team of people working towards a shared goal (or interest or dream) you can reap the benefits of the entire network.

When you rely on the network, you're tapping into something called "duplication." As a budding entrepreneur, I figured out that the power of duplication is really just a function of time. As a teen, I acquired customers in my neighborhood who allowed me to mow and landscape their yards for the summer. I wasn't old enough to drive and it wasn't possible for me to mow all of the yards myself, so I hired some of my friends to do the actual work and I split the money with them. This allowed me to obtain more customers, mow more yards, but most importantly to make money from my network even when I wasn't working. In other words, this allowed me to reap the rewards of duplication. I was generating income based on the original act of creating a network of customers, not from actually doing the work myself.

Of course, before technological advances the dream of creating beach money wasn't truly possible. If networkers wanted to move to the beach and collect their residual, their business would eventually dry up because of their lack of contact and communication with their team. What's more, past limitations of technology prohibited professional networkers from working virtually, much less moving to a beach and collecting income. Today, technology has become a means to heighten social contact, stay engaged with family and friends, connect to online groups and communities, and maintain awareness of news and information streaming to and from a network that has swept the world and revolutionized communication as we know it: the Internet.

Today the difference between connecting with someone down the block and with someone half-way around the world is so slight that it opens opportunities once only dreamed of. Social media abounds, and online programs allow us to maintain face-to-face contact with someone anywhere, anytime. Because we're embedded in an age of hyper connectivity, the complexion of the network marketing industry, once so contingent on personal contact, has also changed. You no longer have to be tied down to a single city to bolster retention and mitigate attrition on your team. Today you can teleconference into team meetings from anywhere around the world. Don't get me wrong. Nothing takes the place of personal contact, and you should try to get in front of your team as much as possible. Only, ensure you use technology for all that it's worth. It has, after all, put the "network" in network marketing, allowing more freedom and flexibility than ever before, and presenting today's network marketer with a previously unforeseen and invaluable gift: the ability to be "virtual."

Because the world runs on a virtual network, real beach money is more than a dream. For many, it has become a way of life. I demonstrated this a few years ago when I took a three-month vacation to a beach in Mexico. While I was there I ran my entire business virtually with the exception of attending major company events. During those three months (of bliss) my income actually grew by 30 percent. And, while I didn't take that time completely off, it allowed me to do three things: be physically removed from my business; enjoy my time on the beach; and grow my income. While I could have taken three months off and just earned "beach money," I chose to put in the small amount of time it takes to create a virtual business, and I was able to see the benefits from the beach. It was easy—no, it was more than easy—it was simple. I was already using many of the tools that allowed me to work virtually, and the new ones I discovered were so user-friendly that I started implementing them immediately.

Anyone who knows me, knows that I love to travel. Why else would I be in the network marketing industry? Seeing the world and its many facets and cultures, languages and traditions, is relevant, enriching and, to be honest, one of the things I live for. So, figuring out how to travel and at the same time run my business were critical to obtaining the lifestyle I desired. Many of the tools and techniques I'm about to show you were unavailable or were incredibly expensive just a few years ago. But today they're key components to making your business virtual.

The Three Rules of Being Mobile

First, there are three simple but crucial rules to follow to ensure your business has a sound foundation. When you build up your team, you want it to stand firm every step of the way and not crumble from the weight of stress, and lack of communication. Successful leaders return to the fundamentals of team building time and time again, and it is my hope that when you read these rules, you repeat them, understand them, know them, and pass them on to every member of your team to do the same. Knowing and implementing these rules will guide you on your journey to making your business virtual and will pay great dividends to the success of your business. These rules are really a demonstration of how one's character and resolve can make a lasting influence on business. Without further ado, here they are:

Rule #1: Stay Connected: The anchor of your virtual business is your mobile device. This is how you stay connected with your team. You cannot be a leader of your organization if you cannot send and receive messages from your phone. If you're not connected, your team will lose motivation and interest, or they'll look for another leader or pursue another opportunity to fill the void of your absence.

Rule #2: Be Available: Staying connected means being available. This is crucial to how you're viewed not only by your customers, but also by your representatives and distributors. Wherever you are, anyone on your team at any time should be able to contact you for advice, questions, updates, event news and emergencies. That means you must have a smart phone with unlimited text and minutes, which has the ability to send and receive email from wherever you are. Today, several of my top producers run their businesses almost completely from their mobile phones. They know the value of staying connected, even when they travel. Which brings up another point about establishing and maintaining a connection with your team: if you choose to travel internationally, you need a phone that will work in international markets. Everyone within my organization knows that I am always available. Now you may be thinking that you wouldn't want to be reachable *all the time*, and that doing so would have repercussions on your personal life. Rest assured, you're still allowed to protect your time and privacy, and knowing the difference between calls and emails, which are time sensitive and require an immediate response, is key. Your team and customers need to know that if something comes up that is important you will be available.

Rule #3: Be Responsive: Whether you're responding at once, or you're responding within the next several hours, you must be responsive. One of the benefits of this industry is that we have control over the time we spend working. Having time freedom in your business also means that there will be circumstances when a typical employee who goes home at 5:00 p.m. may not take a "work" call—but *you must take that call*. You never know who may need you or what the issue may be, but if you don't answer or respond it could cost you a customer or a distributor; and over time, that can become a barrier to your own success. To this day, people often respond to my emails and calls with "Wow! You got back to me so fast," or "Wow! I didn't think I would reach you." When I hear that, it's almost like the person is saying, "You take your business seriously and I am glad I am doing business with you, and I thought you would probably not have the time to help me." Being responsive means you should always return calls or messages in a timely manner, no matter who it is, no matter how mundane, no matter how much it may conflict with your schedule. As a leader, you cannot allow the misconception that you are "too important" to return calls and messages from customers and team members. Not every call requires an immediate response, and you will have to make those decisions for yourself. But I hope I have made my point here. Even when I am "off," I am available. This mindset will pay huge dividends for your business and your credibility.

Ways to Communicate

Now that we've covered the rules of being mobile, let's look at ways to communicate. Being available on your mobile device is just the beginning of being "mobile." Not only is my mobile device an extension of my voice and credibility, it has become my top method of communicating to my entire team via group text. I have several groups built into my phone that I can text at the press of a button. Most service providers now are limiting you to 10 recipients per text, so you have two options:

> **Option #1:** You can find a phone or service provider that doesn't limit group texts.

Option #2: You can buy a phone that will allow you to download an app that allows you to send group texts and bypass the set limits the service provider imposes.

I have opted for an app to send my group text messages, and have built the following groups into my phone:

- **Leaders:** My top performers, who will, in turn, forward appropriate texts to their organizations.

- **Local market:** Customers or distributors who are in my local market.

- **Other markets by city:** I highly advise having groups built city by city so you can send details, updates or messages about *their* local events.

- **All distributors:** This group contains every distributor in my entire organization.

- **All customers:** This group will have all customers I am communicating with.

- **Leaders from other teams:** This is a list I use to let other teams or leaders know information that may be company-specific. I get several "thank you's" from people on this list for sharing information even though I don't directly benefit from their efforts; however, because it builds bonds among the entire company, it is good business.

Now, it goes without saying that texting your organization doesn't replace human contact. Using a group text as your only form of communication with your team will get you nowhere. In life and in business I have seen people choose the "path of least resistance." And some may believe that solely communicating via group text fulfills the requirement of communicating with their representatives and customers. But it doesn't! Texting is just the beginning of staying in contact with your organization. That said, texting definitely has its benefits. I like it because it's one of the fastest forms of communication, and it's invaluable when you want to promote something last minute but are physically incapable of doing so with everyone in your business. Texting is also efficient for communicating with large numbers of people who you would not normally communicate with; this is effective for leaders with teams that contain members well in to the hundreds or thousands.

After I send a group text, I personally follow up with key leaders about the importance and relevance of the text I just sent out. This ensures they understand the value and meaning of the message and it also aligns us on what to say to the team on my behalf. Remember, sending out a group text does not mean everyone is going to respond or participate to what you just sent out. So, it's important that you make every effort to let key members of your business get the word out. I should also stress that you should make it clear to new people on your team who oversee smaller organizations that they cannot just forward your group texts, and use that as their sole method of communication. I always inform every new leader I come in contact with that to be successful I had to personally call and communicate with my entire team until I reached hundreds of customers and distributors. Today, I still personally communicate with up-and-coming leaders to make sure each responds to the most important information and training that is time-sensitive and critical to their business.

Texting Dos & Don'ts

Whatever you do, the first rule in sending a text to your team is to never over text! It's good form not to send more than one message a week to your entire group. Of course, it doesn't hurt to occasionally send a message more than once a week to specific groups or geographic areas to promote an event or recognize achievement. But remember, many people on your team will not be as serious or committed as you are to the business, and you don't want to bombard them by sending group text messages every day. This is why it is important to divide your groups, because it allows you to send only messages that are completely relevant to people and it keeps them from asking, "Why am I getting this?" "This doesn't apply to me" or "Why does this person text me so much?" That said, here a few examples of what is important to text:

- **Specific events:** Make sure they are relevant to the group you are texting.

- **Recognition:** This stimulates activity or focuses on something you are trying to promote. I also call this Hot News; it provides opportunities for your team to be recognized for a promotion or attaining another level of achievement. (Don't go overboard on this one.)

- **Deadlines**: Registration time periods for major events, contests or promotions.

- **Last-minute reminders:** This is relevant for major webinars, events or conference calls. I like texting last minute because it acts like an alarm to participate in whatever it is you are promoting.

- **Personal calls-to-action:** These are texts that seem like they have been sent directly to one person, even though it went to an entire group. For example: "Today Ben and Katie qualified for the new contest, have you qualified yet?" Or "We have more than 300 people registered for tonight's webinar. Have you registered yet?" In other words, the person feels like that text was addressed only to them and not to the entire group. People do not like to feel like they are being herded in groups.

For every texting must, there are also "must-not's." Here are few examples of things not to text:

- **Random events:** Events that are irrelevant to specific markets.

- **Duplicated texts:** Sending the same text or event over and over.

- **Cross-wired texts:** Sending customers topics that may be business-related.

- **Non-specific messages:** Too many texts to people who are not as focused on the business as you are.

- **Demanding texts:** Messages that have a "do this or else" mentality, or have a negative tone.

- **Impersonal texts:** Texts that seem impersonal, i.e., "Date, time and location of a major event" or "*Everybody* needs to get two more sales by this Friday for us to hit our goal!" This is a text that makes a person feel herded or irrelevant because you didn't reach out to them personally.

Building Your Mobile List

Ok, so you've accepted texting as an excellent method of communication to build your virtual business, and to keep in contact with your team, with the following caveats: you use good judgment; you don't let texting replace personal communication, and you always follow up with leaders after every major text to reiterate your message to the team. So, how do you obtain everyone's mobile number? One of the best places to get mobile numbers (and email addresses, for that matter) is at live events. Whether it's a presentation or training, whenever I run a live event I make sure I have a sign-in sheet at the welcome table. I ask guests to print neatly and to include their name, email and mobile number. This way I can build a mobile text list for that specific geographic area. I also immediately add new people into a list that best suits them as soon as I sign them up or whenever I meet them at events. If I collect business cards at events I plug them into my text lists after the event. As soon as I return from live events, I add these new members to my cell phone and to their appropriate group or category. I realize it may be tempting to put this type of follow-up on the back burner, but maintaining good communication lists are vital as your team begins to grow.

Sending Email

Obviously another form of mobile communication, and the most well-known, is email. Email has been around for decades and everyone on the planet is wired in; however, because of such widespread use, email has also been a hot spot for spam, forwarded messages, advertisements and unwanted communication. As a result, sending email may not be the best method of reaching your team. Due to the lack of open rates for emails these days I am only going to spend a little bit of time here.

One of the reasons email can be a strategy for you is that gathering email addresses along with other information online, like phone numbers, via a website, can help you build a database that you can use with other forms of communication, like texting. At the same time, building a website for your team really isn't necessary until you have several hundred or even several thousand people. When you reach that point, having a website will allow you to get announcements out, provide training content, share success stories and even provide team recognition. It's much easier to build an effective group text list as your team grows, than it is to build a team website.

The two most popular email management programs are *iContact* and *Constant Contact*. (Each has pros and cons, and it will be best if you evaluate the prices and differences of the services they offer.) They both have the most important feature which is the ability to put an opt-in box on your website that will allow you to collect information from people in your organization. If your company has back office technology or software that allows you to communicate directly to your team through the company system, then you may be able to eliminate the email communications systems I just referenced. A few years ago I would have preferred using email, but now I would much rather use texting to communicate.

If you choose to communicate via email, adhering to a few simple rules will provide failsafe guidelines much like I shared for text messaging. However, you can do more with emails than you can with text messaging. Here are a few examples of what I like to do with email newsletters:

- **Use a Branded Email Template:** Brand your team name or image and give an identity to your cause; but don't spend too much time on this. You don't need to change your brand often. Just make a template and stick with it.

- **Use Video Messages:** Attach a video to your email every now and then to make your messages more personal and to bring variety to your communication.

- **Use Photos of Team Members or Company Events:** Take photos at company events whenever you can. Sharing photos of your leaders can be used for recognition and promotion in your emails. You can also grab photos off of social media sites for this purpose.

- **Don't Make Them Too Long:** People have short attention spans when it comes to email these days, so just highlight your main objectives and keep them short and simple.

Phone Blasts

Another way of communicating with my team that reaches more people than I can personally is by voice blasting or call blasting. This is a form of voice broadcasting that allows you to upload a database of names and numbers and then record a message that will be sent to everyone on the list just like a personal phone call. Companies that provide this service generally bill in 30-second increments, so time your message to use the entire 30 seconds so you aren't paying for wasted time. Follow the same guidelines as we have previously discussed for texting. The company I use is called www.callemall.com. They have the best prices and a very intuitive platform for sending voice broadcasts. Occasionally, in lieu of sending an email or text, I'll use a phone blast to convey a more personal message to my team. Because I don't use this service often, it carries more importance to my team when they hear this type of message. I also use it for urgent, last minute, announcements, because it is the most direct form of communication without having to physically call everyone.

The Worldwide Webinar

Webinars are a godsend to the network marketer. They have been key in helping me maintain a virtual business when I am travelling around the world. When I lived in Mexico on the beach, I used webinars to train, share information and stay in contact with my team. Webinars have also helped me launch new international markets. By far, this is one of my favorite technology applications. When I started in this industry, webinars didn't exist; then they were available, but you had to be on the phone and on the computer at the same time. Remember when I said that some people like to take the path of least resistance? Well, getting them on the phone *and* their computer at the same time is not easy; it means more of a commitment from the prospect or customer. But today webinar technology has evolved and customers and representatives just need to be on their computer. Some can even watch and listen to a webinar from a mobile device like an iPad! As a result, it's very easy to get someone in any time zone around the world to virtually sit down with you any time. This allowed me to build my business with sales presentation webinars and train new team members from Mexico while I was on vacation collecting beach money. It also gave me the ability to communicate with teams in several countries at their specific time zones either with pre-recorded webinars or a live webinar. There are several companies that provide webinar services, and they are changing rapidly so do your research and choose the most cost-effective solution for the size of your business and the size of your webinars. Here are the ways I use webinars for my business:

- **Run Opportunity or Sales Presentations:** You can present on a live webinar or many services will allow you to play a pre-recorded webinar on demand or at a specific time. You can also have team members do this for you when you're unavailable. This is the main way I leverage the webinar system, and I frequently use it to my advantage to help start new markets, so I don't have to spend time or money traveling to that market until the time is right.

- **Run Training:** Train your teams in different time zones and in different cities at the same time by creating training content and using the webinar to bridge the distance gap.

- **Team Meetings:** If you want more of a personal touch than email or a conference call, you can run a powerful team webinar to blend announcements, updates and strategic information.

Conference Calls

I don't use conference calls nearly as much as I used to before webinars came along. However, in some markets and countries I work with people who don't have the ability to view webinars because they don't have the Internet or their Internet is too slow, so I have to schedule conference calls to run presentations or training. That said, today my primary use of conference calls is for team meetings and announcements. I thrive on the energy and enthusiasm of people gathered on a crowded line from many places around the country or around the world. There really isn't another medium that shares this type of excitement. That's why I *love* using conference calls for major announcements or special promotions. You can really create a buzz by creating a "Last-Minute Emergency Conference Call," peaking your team's anticipation and interest, and they can call in from anywhere so they don't need to plan ahead to be on the call. I also use this as my main form of live communication with my entire organization. Because I don't hold too many conference calls, the ones I do host draw a big group because my team knows it's *important*. Other leaders run weekly team conference calls, which is fine to do especially if there are exciting events happening in your organization that you can share with the entire team. This also works well if you have a market that is exploding with growth and you want to spread some of that energy to your other markets that may not be getting the same results. I will often let a leader or up-and-coming new member from a hot market share with the entire team to spread the buzz. My conference calls usually follow the same pattern:

- **Welcome:** Start the call with the right tone; be high-energy and enthusiastic.

- **Introduction:** Use this time to edify the speaker properly.

- **Message:** Your presentation or your team meeting content.

- **Testimonials:** Share success stories of people doing what you shared in your message.

- **Wrap-up:** This is your "close" if you are presenting with a call-to-action. If you are hosting a team call, use the wrap-up for major announcements, contests or objectives for the upcoming week.

Selling and Presenting with Your Mobile Device

Using your mobile device for communication is not the only thing you have the ability to do as a Mobile Networker. Today we also have the ability to sell and present to customers on your mobile devices. Several companies now have Smart Phone applications that have presentations, trainings and videos for you to share with prospects or team members. If your company does not have an application with this information readily accessible, it does not mean that you cannot transform your mobile device into a sales tool. There are apps and programs out there that will convert presentations into multiple video formats or into images that you can scroll through on your device. I recommend having at least your company's presentation in one format on all of your mobile devices. Some mobile devices may not play regular videos from the Internet that you may be able to access from a computer. You never know when you will have the opportunity to present and there might *not* be an Internet connection (like on a flight). So take a PowerPoint and convert it to a format that your device will be able to show. If your device won't play a PowerPoint presentation, convert the slides to JPEG images and then click through them like a photo album. Just Google the format you're trying to convert and the format you are trying to get to, along with the type of device you're using. This should give you plenty of resources to make your device effective even when you don't have Internet access. All you need is the ability to share your products or opportunity wherever in the world you may be, which should be a top priority for a true mobile networker.

Mobile Applications

There are many applications available for smart phones that you can use to grow your mobile business. You don't need to download every business and productivity application from the App Store, but I have found several useful applications that you can use effectively. Here are some of my favorites that I would definitely download as soon as you can:

1. **Group Text Apps:** There are several group text apps you can download that will allow you to send group text messages to specific lists. This will also allow you to bypass limitations by your service provider on the maximum amount of people you can text with one message. I currently use Group Text, but when you use this service all of the recipients can see the numbers you sent the message to which I do not like. The other apps out there are not as user friendly and have issues with freezing the phone. Stay tuned to my website for updates on the products and services I am using to communicate.

2. **The Mobile Networker:** This is the only app built specifically for Network Marketers, and is a great tool for managing your prospects, setting reminders, and to help with productivity. It is much easier to use and more intuitive than a generic contact manager like Salesforce. I highly recommend downloading this app if you are serious about your business.

3. **Seesmic Ping:** This app will let you post on all of your social media sites at one time, so you can save time and get your posts out faster.

4. **Skype:** This is my favorite app for travelling abroad. This allows you to stay in touch with your team and customers no matter where you are in the world. It also allows you to communicate with your International customers and team members from your own backyard.

5. **Chat Apps:** There are several apps online that you can download that will let you chat with people for FREE just like a text message regardless of your rate plan or service provider. This comes in handy if you have teams internationally or if you are travelling abroad.

Outsourcing

One of my favorite business books is "The 4-Hour Work Week" by Timothy Ferris. If you want to get more in depth information on many aspects of running a virtual business and being mobile, I highly recommend reading this book. One of the things I learned from Ferris was about "outsourcing" tasks that I didn't have time to do or that I did not have the expertise to do. My favorite outsourcing site is Elance. Elance is a website where you can literally post just about any type of job or task and have people from other countries "bid" to win your job. The wages are much more competitive for technology, design and writing in other countries around the world, which allows you to complete a job on a budget and get it done very quickly. Here are some tips I have learned from my many experiences on Elance:

1. **Choose someone with a work history:** On Elance you can see someone's previous work and the feedback previous customers left for them, along with their total earnings on the site. I would never choose someone with no history, no matter how good they appear.

2. **Beware of extremely low bids:** If your job is not a quality sensitive job, then this may not be as big a factor, but if you need something done right or something done quickly, then *do not* choose the lowest bid. Look at all the bids and try to find one that is reasonable, but in line with the other bids you have received on your project.

3. **Don't pay for your job postings:** Some services allow you to "sponsor" a job or "highlight" a job, which means you pay a small fee to have your job listed above other people's jobs in the category of work you are seeking. I have never done this, and have gotten many bids for every job I have posted, and have always gotten good quality work.

4. **When you post your job, ask for examples of work that are *specific* to your job:** You will find that most freelancers will respond to jobs with a generic message and attach their entire portfolio. When I post jobs, I ask for two to three specific examples of the *exact* work I am looking for them to perform. If the bids come in without that information, you can be sure they never read your entire posting and just replied with a generic response based on the category of work you were looking for. If you see someone's work you like, then ask for specific examples relating to your project.

Elance.com is a good resource, and I have used them for several years for the following:

- Designing websites
- Lead capture pages
- Brochures
- Posters
- Flyers
- Formal announcements
- Facebook templates
- Twitter backgrounds

- Written transcriptions of recorded trainings or events

There are many people out there who can help you with your projects and meet your deadlines. Today, there's no need to try to put together a flyer on your own to promote a major event. You can visit Elance or other freelance websites, and get someone to do it for incredibly low and competitive rates. What's more, it will be done by a professional and, more importantly, *look* professional.

Realizing Your Virtual Business

Now, thanks to technology, we're living in the era of the virtual business. And communication tools are only getting better! Thanks to webinars, texting, email and websites, the network marketer can fulfill the dream of beach money, all while maintaining contact with his or her team and continuing to build a strong global business. As a result, more and more people are attaining financial and time freedom, and are raising the ceiling of their expectations, all the while building a network of associates who are also reaping the rewards of truly being mobile.

8

You Are Your Brand

*T*hey say, "You are what you eat." The analogy that what you consume reflects your overall health and well-being is not a new one. But it remains relevant. In this chapter, we'll discuss a similar parallel targeted at expanding and revealing who you are to your business: "You are what you do." This industry gives you the ability to create a brand for yourself, and that brand can be shaped, sculpted and refined into whatever identity you choose. With the assortment of media tools at your disposal, you can create a brand around what you do that will allow people to associate who you are with your accomplishments and your character.

In other words, you are your brand. Actually, it's more accurate to say that your reputation is your brand. What do people think about you? Can they relate to you? Are you a charismatic, innovative and a trustworthy leader? Does your team believe in you? By working to help others reach their goals, you can create a reputation that makes you seem very approachable. Living a fulfilled and inspired life is something that will attract people in any language and in just about any country around the world. Having an identity that people want to emulate and that inspires them will allow you to open new markets around the world and grow your business on a much larger scale.

While social media is important to your online reputation and brand, we will focus on what your objectives should be for creating a reputation for yourself online and offline. We will cover social media more in depth later on in the book. One of the great opportunities the Internet gives you is the ability to *brand* yourself *how you* choose to, rather than living an identity that someone else has given you or assigned to you. The methods and strategies we use in this chapter can also lead into what we discussed about creating your team's identity and culture in an earlier chapter since many of the ways you communicate your culture to your team are by using the Internet and of course social media. Since your organization is a direct reflection of you, it is important to decide how you want to brand yourself so you can also use these tools to create an identity for your team or organization.

First thing's first, you must be a product of your product. That means you must make whatever product or service you are selling or promoting part of your daily routine and an integral part of your life. It's crucial that you fall in love with your products or services, and find new ways to incorporate them into your day-to-day activities. I don't care what you sell; you must keep your products in mind as you carry out your everyday errands, tasks, meetings and events. If what you sell or represent is "out of sight and out of mind," you will miss opportunities to recruit, train and prospect. On the other hand, if you consistently use your products and services and if they are on your mind as you go throughout your daily activities, you will encounter prospects each day who will almost fall into your lap because they are attracted to your belief in what you do or the attitude you have about your life.

I am often asked, "Why are you so happy?" Let me translate what this question really means: "How can I find the happiness and fulfillment I see in you for myself?" If someone asks you this, it's a reflection that you have done something right, that you are blessed, and it's your responsibility to not only provide an answer, but to give them a guide to achieving fulfillment themselves. When I am approached with this question, I use it as an opportunity to create a bond and build a friendship with this person, and it's very likely they will become a customer or a member of my team because they're already influenced by my attitude and my lifestyle.

How you incorporate your products and services into your life also gives you the ability to train. When I spend time with new people in my business, I emphasize the perks and benefits of my products during my daily routine. This gives me the ability to cast a vision for them by emphasizing the gifts and advantages my products have given me. Whenever I am spending time with people I often find ways to share experiences or stories that I have had because of the products. I also showcase the lifestyle and freedom that my business allows me to have. I don't just brag about my success, financial and otherwise; rather I tell them about the lives I have changed and the experiences and memories I have created for myself and others around me. This is all part of creating your brand and image in the eyes of your team.

Also, remember your business should be open 24 hours a day, 365 days a year. That doesn't mean you have to work 24 hours a day without taking time off. It means you should never turn your business off. You should always be aware of what is going on during business hours and after business hours. It may not sound like fun if you can never turn your business off; but the reality is that if you master this technique, you will be a "master in the art of living."

One of my mentors always used this quote, which you may be familiar with:

> *"The master in the art of living makes little distinction between his work and his play, his labor and his leisure, his mind and his body, his education and his recreation, his love and his religion. He hardly knows which is which. He simply pursues his vision of excellence at whatever he does, leaving others to decide whether he is working or playing. To him he is always doing both."*
>
> *–LP Jacks*

This quote simply conveys that you should love what you do. When the opportunity presents itself, be a "networker." If you can network, then network, whether it's during or after business hours. If I'm having dinner out, for instance, and the person serving me is an intelligent, well-spoken individual, it's a safe bet that I will get their number by the end of the night. I make a connection with everyone I come in contact with, and try to be as contagious as possible, sending out positive energy so everyone around me wants to know what I do. That's what gives me the perfect lead-in to get someone's contact information when the time is right. Make your attitude and energy conducive to meeting people. Aim to be the person everyone is curious about, and make everyone wonder what you do.

Many people are not happy at the end of the work day, and consequently, when they get home the highlight of their day may be their favorite TV show, or even hitting the local happy-hour with friends. Most people assume that *we* should all be tired and worn out from the "day at the office." But if you follow the guidelines in this book, you'll set yourself apart from everyone else who has to go through the grind of everyday life.

> *Decide how you want to brand yourself.*

If you're at a job right now that you don't like, that is unfulfilling and unsatisfying, and you know with every ounce of your being that it will not lead to financial freedom or more time with your family, then do this: when you're not at work, completely focus on the lifestyle you want to create rather than the lifestyle you currently have. Focusing on creating your new brand is the time when you get a chance to be the "you" that you want to be, and not the "you" that people expect you to be based on your current circumstances. You need to carry yourself this way regardless of whether you are with your team or if you are with complete strangers. Embracing the identity of the lifestyle you choose is just the beginning of your brand as it relates to your future.

Personally, I find this attitude and personality is easier to have when you are surrounded by people on your team or involved with your company. When you're around at least two other people who do what you do, it gives you a bullet proof vest around your confidence. People are much more comfortable living their life with a positive and optimistic business outlook when they are around others who have the same values and beliefs. And while you'll obviously spend time away from the people on your team, and people around you may not know who you are or what you do, they are still watching and observing how you react or respond to situations. This is your chance to be the person you want to be, the person you believe in and project, the person you say you are when you describe your interactions to your team and organization. The key is to be that person regardless if someone is watching you or not. This is the true test of an ultimate networker. Do you act the same when you are alone as you do when your team or organization is around you? If you can answer, "yes" to that question, you are one step ahead in this chapter of establishing your brand; because your brand doesn't sleep in this business. It's important to remember, whether you are just getting started or if you have thousands on your team, make every attempt to be the person you say you are when you teach and train your new people, and be that person when they are not watching.

What you do and who you are has an impression on others, and you never know when the opportunity might present itself to expand your organization or start a new market when you are out and about, as we touched on in an earlier chapter about prospecting strangers. Also, be aware and constantly keep in mind how you appear to your team, no matter how big or how small the gathering.

The Social Persona

You need to take advantage of the new age of social media and information to create a persona for you that may, at times, seem bigger than life. I don't mean that you should be boastful; I just mean that every once in a while you need to be the "light" in someone's day. Be the person most people wish they were instead of the person they actually are. Many people get stuck in the grind and follow the path everyone else follows. That makes it easy for them to tell when someone is not following that path. Whether you're being positive or optimistic, or you carry yourself differently than the majority of people they come across, take this opportunity to set the tone for how your organization views you as their leader.

One of the best ways to communicate with your team and share the lifestyle you want to embody is via social media. While we will cover Facebook and other new forms of social media in a later chapter, I want to focus on some other aspects of online personal branding in this chapter. The underlying goal is to share what you are doing in a non-boastful approach that could have an impact on future customers or prospects, and also on your current organization. The Internet makes it so easy today to create a personality almost out of thin air. The only difference between you and some of the biggest Internet marketers in the world is they have more of an Internet presence. It's easier today to share your story around the globe and in different time zones than ever before, and from the comfort of your own home. Two ways to create and promote your brand online are blogging and posting videos on YouTube.

Blogging

Let's start with blogging because it will give you the best platform to express yourself while creating a brand at the same time. While writing may be more difficult than filming a video, it also provides more visibility on the Internet. Most search engines only search text on the Internet, so it's important that part of your presence online is ad copy or text content that is updated as frequently as possible. Search engines place preference on content that is fresh and updated in their ranking and search results. Without getting into more detail on web search patterns and search engine optimization, I want to provide some tips to start creating your brand online with a blog. The relevance of blogging on the Internet is more powerful today than ever before. Blogging has gotten to be so important that thousands of people make money just from blogging, and even one of the original blogging platforms, WordPress, has become one of the fastest-growing platforms for building new websites on the Internet. My suggestions for your blog are as follows:

1. Set up a blog on one of the popular blogging platforms: WordPress or Blogger.

2. Choose a theme that represents you and the brand you want to create.

3. Write about *relevant* content for your friends, family, prospects, customers and your everyday reader.

4. Discuss the benefits of the lifestyle you are trying to create, such as freedoms, time off, time spent with family, vacations, new purchases, new outlooks on life and powerful quotes.

5. Keep your content fresh: post something on your blog at least once a week and try to be consistent. Even when you're busy, remember to update your blog.

6. Mix up your content with videos, photos and text content. Blogs are much easier for search engines to find content on than social media sites, so if you are posting photos and videos on social sites try to share the same content or similar content on your Blog at the same time.

7. Interview people or link in information from experts on topics you are discussing.

8. Join other blogs and post comments that link back to your blog to get additional followers.

9. Mention current events or newsworthy items that will catch people's attention and that can also help your blog show up on more search engines.

10. Make sure you integrate ad sense or some form of monetization on your blog so you can start to monetize your content in addition to building your brand. Blogger has a very easy platform that integrates Google AdSense since Google owns Blogger. You probably are not going to generate millions from your blog, but it will be some nice

extra money for something that you should be doing anyway to build your brand for your existing business.

I have recently integrated my old blog into my new website just to keep everything in one place and to make my branding more uniform and consistent. However, having your blog separate from your personal website gives an entirely different avenue for people to find you online. Your blog will show up in their search engine as a completely different domain, and if you do not have a personal website yet, this should be your first online presence because it is the fastest and easiest to set up. Try to stay on top of your blog, by making a personal commitment to yourself. This has been something that I have personally not kept up with as much as I should have over the past three or four years. If I had been blogging this whole time, I would have had enough content for another book.

YouTube

Another way of establishing your Internet presence and your global brand is by using YouTube. Remember, content on your videos will not get searched by Internet search engines; they only get searched by the key words associated with that particular video. This isn't as important if you are using your channel primarily to communicate with an audience that is looking for your page specifically or if you are using YouTube to send videos specifically out to your customers or team members. However, if you want people unfamiliar with your business or people who are looking for your particular products or services to be able to find you, then keep in mind that they will find you via the video's key words not the actual content on your video itself. With that being said, let me give you some basic tips on how to build a good YouTube presence online:

1. Don't get three strikes! You may think I am kidding, but this is *very* important! You don't want to wake up one day and find that your YouTube page has been completely deleted. This is what happens after your third strike. I know people who have had this happen to them and they were almost in

tears. So make sure all of your content is original and *don't* use music, photo montages, or any other copyrighted material in *any* of your videos. If you get warned about this three times, YouTube will delete your account and it is very near impossible to get it back up.

2. Make your videos spontaneous. Your videos don't need to be professionally made. People like the feel of something unrehearsed. Obviously, keep your image and brand in mind when you step in front of the camera, but keep the camera rolling whenever possible so you can get natural footage.

3. People love videos with step-by-step instructions, so if you can outline a practical plan, whether you are training or explaining particulars, it will give people a clear direction on how to use it.

4. Keep your videos short and to the point. People have short attention spans and do not want to listen to a bunch of fluff on YouTube. Most videos on YouTube with the biggest viewer numbers are less than one minute. So keep it concise!

5. Try to film at locations or events that people want to hear about or see. I always try to shoot video when I am at a major sporting event or concert that will draw extra views to that particular video. I also put the special event in the title of the video.

6. Create videos for three types of audiences: your team, your customers and your prospects. Make sure you keep your audience in mind when you choose your titles and make sure you are clear who the video is for by using a title specific for that group.

    a. Video topics for team members include product updates, product explanations, event promotions, team updates from events, recognition of achievement, highlights of team events and testimonials of success.

b. Video topics for customers include product benefits, product announcements, product value explanation, how to use products and testimonials of product success.

c. Video topics for prospects include value explanation, benefits explanation, generic success stories, lifestyle benefits of the business, dream-building stories and testimonials.

7. Choose your titles and keywords with purpose. The catchier title the better; make your titles create curiosity. The words you use in your title should be the words that you think people will be searching for. Also, remember that your keywords are the only way people will find your video without going directly to your page, so choose keywords that are most relevant to your company, product, opportunity and, of course, the benefits specific to those areas.

Your Personal Website

If you use the two forms of online branding we just discussed and combine that with what we are going to talk about in the chapter on social media, you will have a very powerful and useful brand presence on the Internet for yourself. One other thing to consider is your personal website; although it is not necessary for you to create a personal website, it can be very inexpensive and take your professionalism to an entirely different level. I get a great amount of satisfaction from giving people my email address and the web domain is my name. People ask me all the time when I give them my email address what I do because I have my own website. It is a great conversation starter, and immediately gives you more professionalism and credibility with your team and your prospects. Even if all you have on your personal website is a bio, a photo, and your contact info, that puts you ahead of most people on the planet. You may be thinking, "Well that sounds great, but how can I create a good looking website that isn't one of those cheap looking, build-it-yourself websites that they promote in all the magazines?" The answer is, yet again, Elance, like we discussed earlier in the book. You can literally get a great looking website built on a WordPress platform which you can integrate with your blog that you can manage without knowing how to program anything. The entire thing can cost you less than $250 dollars on Elance. Here's how to do it:

Step 1: Go to www.Godaddy.com and buy your domain. I suggest using your first and last name if it is available. You will have this for the rest of your life, and who knows what you will use it for in the future. If your name isn't available then try combinations of your name with initials or maybe try a nickname. If you can't find something that you like, then think about one of your favorite words or places and try to incorporate that into a name for your website. You will also need to add a basic hosting account to your domain which will only cost a few bucks a month.

Step 2: Go to www.elance.com, and post a Job for "Graphic Designers to Create a PSD file of your website." PSD is short for a Photoshop file which is a program most designers are familiar with and most Internet programmers can use to turn into an actual website. This is a graphic design project with no programming involved so make sure you are clear about this in your job posting. If all you are doing is a simple one page website, you could probably skip this step and go straight to step number three, but the reason I like to let the designers come up with a design is because they are designers and not all computer programmers are good designers. You should list in the job description what you are using the website for, and what the theme of the website will be or the industry you are in. This step should cost between $100-$200 depending on how many pages you are having them design. If you are doing a one-page website for now, then one thing you can do is just find some websites you like online and give them to the designer you choose and tell them to use the same look and feel. If you are new to this industry, you can start your website with just some photos of you, your contact info and maybe some information about your company or your products. If you are ready for a full-blown website with more information and content, you will need to tell the designer about the subpages the site will have. Once you get the look and feel you are going for, you can proceed to step three.

Step 3: Post a job for "Programmer Needed to Convert PSD design to Website." Most programmers are now using WordPress for personal websites and this type of website is also very easy to add or change content yourself, so that is what I suggest you tell the programmer to use. Give them your GoDaddy login information and the PSD file that your designer created and they should get your design turned into a live site in about a week. This should cost you between $100-$200, depending on how many pages you have in your design. If you choose WordPress, you should be able to use this website for a long time and just go in and freshen up your content from time to time as your business grows. If you are only doing the one-page website, you could just post one job and explain that you need minor web design work and a one-page website built. This should only cost you $100 max. The last one-page website I had built on Elance was only $50 and was very complex.

This book is not about website building, but this simple process I just gave you will give you a virtual business card on the Internet for under $400, and if you are only doing a simple one-page website you could probably do it for under $100. Make sure that you work on your online presence in your off peak hours, which is the time you are not spending recruiting, prospecting, training, or working with your team. Your Internet presence includes everything we have just talked about, and everything we are going to talk about in the chapter on social media. People make a big mistake of spending prime business hours on busy work online. These types of activities can add to your business, but they are what I call "Down Time" activities. These types of activities, along with several of the components of team communication and organization that we have talked about throughout the book, can be done when the important tasks that create real income for you cannot be done. Your "Prime Time" activities are the things that will pay your bills immediately so make sure you focus on: prospecting, selling and presenting during your main business hours.

Make a Commitment

The last thing I want to discuss in regards to your reputation and brand is the concept of jumping around to different companies. First off, if you have already worked with several companies and you feel like you are in the "No Friends Left Club," that is just complete nonsense. I tell people all the time that companies and businesses are kind of like relationships. Just because one doesn't work out doesn't mean that the next one won't. If we gave up on relationships just because one didn't work, then everyone would be single. I'm pretty sure most people out there did not marry the first person they ever dated. That said, it is very important that you make a strong commitment to your company and your products. If you are not completely sold or convinced that your company is the right "permanent vehicle" for your business and financial future, make the decision right now to find a company and stick with it. People who jump around from company to company are the ones who give the industry a bad reputation. It's similar to men or women who jump from relationship to relationship and are never really committed to the one they are in. If you never really make a commitment to your company, how do you know that when you failed, it wasn't your fault? Maybe the company or the product was great, but you never gave it a chance. The same goes for relationships. If you never make a total commitment, you never really know how good the relationship could have been. The only way you can fail in this industry is to quit. So let me make the suggestion that you commit to your company and your products from this day forward and that you *will not quit*. Quitting is the only thing that will keep you from getting everything you want from this industry. So, if you have made this mistake in the past, don't do it again. Make this a fresh start and a new commitment.

You are your brand! If you embrace an attitude about this being your long-term plan and long-term strategy, then people will know that this is the *new* you and that you are the type of person who they will want to work with and be around. I don't believe in the "No Friends Left Club." Remember, just because something didn't work out for you previously, doesn't mean your new experience will end the same way.

You have to believe in what you are representing and what you are promoting. If you have an attitude that "this" opportunity is your future and that this company and the products you are representing are the best out there, then your attitude and belief will be conveyed to your prospects. Your friends and family who may have seen you fail in the past or know that you had a bad experience with another company or product, will be able to find confidence in your newfound commitment. Someone who does *not* support your new business would be just like you *not* supporting your friend who is dating someone new because their previous relationship didn't work out. That doesn't make sense, does it? However, perception, like most people say, "is reality," so make the perception that you are going to be successful and that you are committed to see your business through no matter who or what stands in your way.

The past isn't as important as the present and what you are doing right now is the only thing that matters as long as you are **committed to it!**

9

Social Networking

*T*he key to mastering social media for your business is to understand a very simple philosophy: "Friends first, recruit later." Remember this, and you're on your way to getting the most out of a network that spans continents and connects millions of people worldwide. If you want to build your brand, image, reputation and ultimately your business with social media, you must be friends first. In other words, if you don't build a relationship, it defeats the purpose of "*social*" media. The word "social" itself should tell you the direction you need to go to have success on this platform. It is not called "selling" media; if it was then people would not be using it for their everyday life because the average person does not want to be "sold." If all you do is build a page or profile to sell, market or promote, you will not have very much of a following and you will not build your business.

In this chapter, I will discuss the do's and don'ts of social media as a broad topic rather than covering each social media website, because most of these concepts can be applied to multiple websites, services, forums and blogs, so as the social media landscape changes, you can use these theories on whatever platform you choose.

Social Media Gone *Wrong*

Today more people are using social media for their business than ever before. Unfortunately, they're using it the wrong way! Often, when I'm on online, I see someone (many times that person is very new to the industry) blatantly promoting their business or products the wrong way via social media. So let's start by talking about what *not* to do.

"Friends first, recruit later." The biggest social media mistake is to over-post or over-sell. This is the number one way to get people to "unfriend" you, "unfollow" you or "block" you. In my opinion, one of the reasons why Facebook made it and MySpace didn't, is that MySpace was too commercial. On MySpace, you could put banners and other commercial advertisements on your profile, but the problem was that people didn't like seeing them every time they visited your profile. Facebook has been really smart from the beginning and they've made it easy for their members to unfriend or block people that they no longer wish to interact with on Facebook. If somebody posts something you don't like or don't want to see, you can literally "one-click" block them and you will never have to see anything they ever do on Facebook ever again. When this happens, it doesn't even notify the person that they have been blocked. You might be thinking, "Oh my gosh, I may not have any friends left, everybody may have blocked me." Yes, that's possible, so stop doing what you're doing to get people to block you. Which means *stop* over-posting, *stop* spamming and *stop* over-selling—these are the biggest turn offs for most people using social media. Here are the most important things to remember:

1. **Don't Over-post:** We don't need to know every time you do something throughout your day. "I left my house. Now I'm in my car. Now I'm on my way to do a presentation. I just left a presentation, man that was fun. Also, tonight I might go to sleep. I'm still awake; I'm not asleep yet. But tomorrow I'm gonna be excited when I wake up. Oh, it's morning, I'm awake." That's a slight exaggeration, but if you over-post, people will block you. This also includes posting too much about your company or products. If you look at my Facebook page, I post no more than one company-related message per week. I know you're excited about your company and your products, but remember this is *social*

media not *"selling"* media. So, tone down your business messages. I will explain what you should say later in this chapter.

2. **Don't Over-sell:** This means don't post your websites in a purely promotional post. Also, don't post your websites on comments, photos, or places where you are just trying to get someone to click on your website and buy. Recently I discovered company websites, which generate "official" company emails have been listed as spam on most email servers because of the amount of people spamming company websites on social media pages. As a result, this can negatively affect your entire company, as recipients will not be able to receive "official" company email because it goes into their spam folder. In today's social media landscape when someone does things the wrong way, word spreads fast, and that can actually affect your entire company. No one wants to be sold in a place where they are connecting with friends and family. So, if you're posting websites, you're actually the modern-day *spammer*. Many new representatives and distributors get so excited when they first sign up that they post all over social media about their new business, products, and services, and that sends up red flags to every potential prospect they know. Once people see all of your selling messages when you start trying to prospect them, they will already know what you are calling about, and they will probably say something like; "Oh, is this that THING you posted about on Facebook last week?" Even if you post a message about a product or service that has changed your life, if you put a website at the end of the post, *everyone* knows you are *trying to sell*! Don't try to sell blatantly in your posts, because people will feel like you're forcing it on them. Rather, post something without selling and have someone ask you about it, because then you're just sharing your life with people, and if you're letting them come to you, then those people don't feel like they're being sold. You can say the same thing and just

leave your website off, and that alone makes a huge difference.

3. **Don't Use Logos or Trademarks:** I also recommend not using your company's trademarks, logos or trade names on any of your pages or on any of your posts. Those names are copyrighted, they're trademarked, and you don't want novice representatives or distributors posting things that could create legal issues for your company. In fact, if it were me, I would never post anything with my company's name in any type of promotional or sales-y post that could be misconstrued or exaggerated. Just err on the side of caution and stay away from using any of this specific information in your social media posts. This also means if you form groups or communities, don't name the groups with your company or product names, because you don't want people to confuse that for an "official" company page, group, or forum. In other words you don't want someone creating a group that a prospect or regulator could perceive as an "official" company page that could create liability issues for your company. Most companies are creating policies and procedures around these ideas, so this will also save you from possible reprimand from your company.

4. **Don't invite:** Prospects don't want to be invited to events or presentations through group posts, banners or mass messages. This is something I don't see very often, but it definitely doesn't work. If something is that *important* then it deserves a personal invitation not a *mass* message. Make sure you explain this to your new people because most people just assume that new members are going to know how to invite properly and assume they're going to do it all the right way. So a new person may think, "I have 500 friends on Facebook, I'll just post that I'm having a Grand Opening as an event on Facebook, and then I'll have 500 people there." Once I was talking to a new person on my team, and I was excited about them being on board so I called them and said, "I'm excited you're having your Grand

Opening this weekend, and I'm sure so-and-so met with you and went over what to expect?" They replied, "Well, no, but I know exactly what to do, and guess what? I'm going to probably have like 200-300 people at my Grand Opening because I posted an event on Facebook and I have like 500 friends, I'm sure at least half of them will come." I was thinking to myself, "Try zero of them will come." I had to burst his bubble and explain this to him, "If you want someone to take this seriously, and if it's important, when you say 'I've got something you need to see, it's important to me,' you're not going to send them a mass message online. When you make it personal then it tells the person that it's important."

5. **Don't Send Apps or Games:** This tip is mostly for Facebook, but it could apply in some other scenarios—don't send games, apps or junk to your friends or address books. Anytime an application or services asks, "Would you like us to access your address book?" you need to stop and think of what the repercussions will be to your reputation and image online and offline. This is also the easiest way to get blocked by your friends and contacts online. When you send someone a game request, and they get that request, they have the ability to block you forever, with the click of one button. So, if you like playing video games, play them on Xbox, and don't play them on Facebook or if you do, then play them alone without inviting all of your contacts to play with you.

So what should you do, now that I've killed all your dreams and ambitions in regards to social media? Maybe you're freaking out right now and saying to yourself, "Oh no, I don't have any friends on Facebook left and I didn't realize it!" It's OK, there's still hope for you and if you haven't done any of this, you are way ahead of the game.

Social Media Gone *Right*

Now that we have discussed the biggest mistakes people make in regards to social media it is time for us to spend some time focusing on exactly what you should be doing. There are several platforms and websites today that make up the social media landscape, and these strategies and suggestions will work in many different situations. Your company or team may have certain rules or restrictions in regard to social media or the Internet so make sure you check with your upline or sponsor before you start using my theories to build your business online.

1. **Support Official Pages:** The most important thing you can do for you and your company with social media is to promote that every customer, representative and distributor "like" your official company Facebook page. In addition to liking your official company page you should also try to post photos and comments on the official company page that can add credibility to your products and opportunity. I use my company's official Facebook page as a closing tool. Have you ever had someone say to you at the end of a presentation "Is this real?" or "Does it really work?" I don't even have to answer that objection anymore, I literally just go to Facebook, I click on my official company Facebook page, which has tons of fans, and I say "Why would all these people like something that ripped them off or wasn't real? They wouldn't, right?" So then I click through some of the people and profiles who are fans, and show them people who have similar interests or a similar background. I also like to point out other people who live in the same city as they do, and I share success stories of top performers and let them see that the people and stories are real. So if everybody is using and supporting your official company Facebook page, then it can be used as a way to close prospects when they have doubts, or to instill confidence in the company or program. In today's communication and information age, if you're ripping

people off, people will find out about it very quickly, and you're not going have tons of people liking you or following you on Facebook and other social media outlets. So this could be one of your best closing tools, if everyone shares stories, photos, videos and testimonials on the Official Company page.

2. **Make a Social Footprint:** Your mission going forward is to try to create a social footprint on the Internet as you pursue your goals, passions, hobbies, or interests and create memories for you and your family. This means whenever you get the chance to share your photos, videos and experiences that represent you and the life you are living, then do so, because it also builds your business at the same time; but do so without mentioning your website and without trying to sell. Instead focus on the life you are living and the life you are trying to create for yourself and your family. If you don't over-do it, people will be drawn to you, especially if they sense a heightened level of energy, positivity and enthusiasm. If they're not attracted to these things, they're probably not the people you are looking to bring into your business anyway. Try to post things about the following categories: lifestyle, health, freedom, success, inspiration, family, and friends. Rotate the things you post about, and you will get much better feedback from your friends and followers. If you only post about one category or one topic on your page, people will stop watching or paying attention. So try to mix it up and get creative. You can use photos, videos, comments, likes, posts, status updates, tweets, audios, quotes, and even share things from other people's pages as you increase your presence and reach through social media. Be active on your own page, but also share and post on your friends, family, team members, and, of course, on your official company page. Have purpose with your posts. Don't just post because you haven't done it in a while. Think about every action on social media before you do it. Some things on the Internet cannot be undone, so

make sure you are careful and think about what you post as you create your social footprint online.

3. **Establish Social Proof:** Make sure you use social media to create "social proof" of all the benefits you are getting from your business or from your products. What I mean by social proof is, just be you, live your life and enjoy your lifestyle and, at the same time, build your brand by including things that have something to do with your business periodically. So think about the following when you're posting: "Am I posting something that can share my lifestyle or results from my business or products?" You should ask yourself: "Is this relevant to people?" Don't overdo it, because if all of your posts are about your business and lifestyle, people will start to tune them out. It's not normal for people to be happy and fulfilled all the time, so when you're having fun and living a full life, it can be contagious, and people will start asking you questions about your lifestyle and about the changes they may be seeing in you. I have recruited 20-30 people over the last year or two, who have come straight to me wanting to know more about what I do. Why? Because my posts were strategically placed, showcasing my lifestyle and the benefits of my product. As a result, I've received messages from people I hadn't seen in 20 years, like this one: "I have no idea what you do, but I want to do whatever it Is, because your life looks amazing." After this, I don't even have to show the presentation because they're already in. When you start getting inquisitive messages from people, don't go straight for the sale and say, "I'm great! And I'm glad you messaged me. I'm going to make you rich! You gotta check out this video and these products!" I keep them at bay, by saying, "Well, thank you for the compliments. I really appreciate it. How've you been? I haven't seen you in forever." You might be saying, "Well, they just told you they want to sign up. Don't you want to sign them up?" Yeah, I want to sign them up, but I don't want to seem needy, desperate, or sales-y. Remember,

people don't want to be sold. So, when you have an opportunity to share your business or product, don't go straight for the sale. I put the ball back in their court by saying, "Yes everything is great, we'll have to talk more about that when we catch up." And if they ask again or say something like, "No really, tell me what you really do." I will respond with something like this, "Well I'm really glad that you want to hear about it, but I want to hear more about you. How are your kids? How's your job? What have you been up to?" Then they almost stop me and say, "No, seriously, tell me what you do." Then it's not me selling them, it's them selling themselves. This brings people's guards down, and they'll listen with open ears and an open mind.

4. **Drip with Social Media:** One of the most important things to understand about using social media is the concept of "the drip campaign." You may recognize the concept of a drip campaign, which is, when you offer small bits of information to prospects over a period of time to build interest and curiosity without overwhelming them or completely presenting to them. The technique behind a drip campaign should be very subtle and deliberate as you make social media posts. Again, don't just post for the sake of posting. There is always a way to incorporate your business or lifestyle into your posts without coming across like you are selling. If you are successful with this method, you will attract people to you that will ask you the right questions. Once this starts to happen it will open windows of opportunity that allow you to discuss your products or business with them without forcing it on them. Here are some ways that you can "drip" using social media:

    a) **Ask questions:** If you ask questions, and get creative, you can engage people on your page. If you attract people to your social media site, and you ask compelling questions, people will start interacting with you and will visit your page more often. Ask questions about anything other than controversial issues. The last thing you want to do is post something controversial and create a war of words among your followers. I like to post questions that seem more like surveys, but at the same time share the level of success I am having with my company. For instance: "My company is sending me on a free trip to Vegas! What's your favorite hotel in Vegas?" Did you catch how I promoted the opportunity and asked a fun question at the same time? Some people would just post something about "going to Vegas" or "getting a free trip" and leave out the opportunity to ask, "What's your favorite hotel?" Others would just say something like "I'm going to Vegas, what is your favorite hotel?" They would leave out the opportunity to promote their success and their company by not mentioning "my company is sending me on a free trip to Vegas!" This misses an opportunity to interact with your page and get people talking about your trip, while, at the same time, making them wonder how you got a free trip in the first place, and also make them curious about what company you work for. If they know you have a typical office job, then some people may ask you when your day job started sending you on FREE vacations.

Even if they don't actually ask the question on your page or to you personally, they are definitely wondering to themselves how you got a free trip to Vegas. I'm very subtle about how I mix promotional material with posts. I don't want to just talk about my company or my products in every post. However, when you can, drop a subtle promotional segment inside a question that gets several people to engage in conversation on your page—that's advertising that money can't buy. I had more than 80 comments on that one Vegas post alone. You also don't have to get a free trip to Vegas to ask a question like that. If you receive something from your company, even if it is as simple as free product, turn it into a question that highlights your achievement in a subtle way.

b) **Comment selectively:** I try to comment on my team's pages and my friend's pages as often as I can, especially to attract more followers to my own page in the process. I look for things that fit with my company or products and the lifestyle we're trying to achieve, even if it isn't related to my business specifically. I will look for people who mention topics like: lifestyle, entrepreneurship, wellness, sales, marketing, business, the economy, the job market, personal development, leadership, or other areas that could fit with my product or services. I find ways to recognize positive statements or trends, and make comments that are complimentary and uplifting. People will notice the attitude and mindset I have as I post on pages, and that will attract others with a positive mindset as potential friends, prospects, or customers. I will also try to post comments specifically on my team-members' pages that will make "their" followers curious and interested in what they are doing as well. This allows you to use your social media skills not only to benefit your personal recruiting efforts, but also your team as they develop their own skills in this area. The benefit of using posts that "drip" on other people's pages is that you didn't have to create the first content yourself. In other words, this gives you a larger canvas to be able to spread your message without having to come up with some catchy way to work your business into your own page updates. For example, a recent post from someone on my team said the following:

"Spent the weekend on personal development." I posted the following comment: "It's obvious you've been doing this for a while now, based on all of the success you are having! Glad we have the opportunity to work together!" This gave me the opportunity to pay them a compliment, and at the same time drop a hint that they have been "successful" at something that will make people wonder what business I am referring to and exactly how "successful" that person has been. This can benefit the person whose page I actually posted on, and at the same time make more people curious about what I do when they see my comment.

c) **Tag people:** Make sure when you tag people in photos that they're actually in the photos. I spend a lot of time removing tags that people have placed of me in photos that I am not actually in. It's OK to mention people in posts when there is not a photo, but make sure you're tagging people appropriately. Tagging puts the information on your page and on other people's pages that you are tagging. Using the @ symbol to tag people in posts on Facebook is a great way to get more eyes on your comments. Don't tag people in every post you make; some people do this way too much. I try to mention a few people a week in the posts I make. I also like tagging people in posts when I am giving recognition to someone in my organization, but if you are recognizing business results, make sure it isn't too business-oriented or that it gives away too much information on that person's page, especially if they are "dripping" on their own followers. You can also use hashtags if you're using Twitter, and even put the hashtags on your Facebook posts as well. Hashtags are # symbol, and on twitter this is a great way to draw interest on certain topics or people. This will pick up a bigger audience for your social media posts on the web. And as social media sites start interacting more with each other, and as more sites share information there will be more opportunities for posts, comments, and tags to show up on search engines and other social media platforms.

d) **Bring value to people:** One great way to establish a "drip" campaign is to bring value to people in your posts and comments. I'm not saying that you need to have a news article with research in every one of your posts, but I will periodically post an interesting story, article, quote, or fact that people may like to re-post or share with their followers that will link back to my original post that could help me attract followers. This also keeps people interested in what you have to say. If all you do is post quotes every day, people will stop paying attention to your quotes in general because you do it too often. If all you do is just post news articles, people will stop following you, because they would prefer to go out and read their own news. However, if you can sprinkle in these types of posts or comments, it will make a follower want to stay on top of the information you are sharing because they think it is relevant, and because it is used sporadically enough not to overwhelm them. Remember, these pages are designed to be "social," so ask yourself if people would be interested in hearing the same information in a social setting.

When I started using social media I did not have the level of success that I have now, and I was probably in a similar place as many of you are today. If you feel like you don't have the lifestyle or the results you want to share on your page currently, you have two options:

- You can post information about the path you are on, and the goals you are working towards which works in a similar way to posting the actual results.

- You can mention people who do have the results you are trying to achieve from time to time, so that people can see those you're surrounding yourself with. This will achieve the same effect as posting information about yourself. I still share my team's photos and stories almost as much as I share my own, so it is not just about me and it shouldn't be just about you.

So if you're not a Top Earner yet, and you haven't achieved the level of success you want, then share other people's photos, other people's experiences, and get out there and take some photos of people making these things happen. Don't use lack of experience, or lack of results as a reason not to follow the tips I have just given you.

e. **Prospecting:** I've lived in several places over my time in the industry, and when I move to a new market, I usually start a team from scratch. Recently when I moved, I only knew one person in the city I moved to, and so one of the things I did to meet new people was to search for local interest groups on Facebook. Find groups that you can be a part of. Find organizations or clubs that you can join. Find school or alumni groups that you should be a part of based on where you went to school. There was a young professional group on Facebook in my local area, and there were about 50 business owners who formed this professional networking group that met once a month. I joined that group and I ended up signing up seven or eight people from that one group of people. Finding group pages on social media sites was one of my best ways of prospecting in the new area. So, if you're a young professional, you can look for young professional groups; if you have a certain business interest or background, there are a lot of alliances, co-ops, organizations, and groups that you can join depending on what demographic you are in or what interests you may have. This is one of the things you can do in your downtime at night, if you can't sleep. If you're excited about your business, go online and look for some of these organizations or groups, so you can join them.

f. **Attract Followers:** I like to build followers on my social pages by leaving comments on sites and blogs that provide the option of sharing the post via social media. This is a great way to attract followers on Facebook or other social sites. Look for the Twitter and Facebook mini boxes on forums, blogs and places where you see information online; these small buttons allow you to link back to your social pages which will show up on the website you are at in some cases in addition to your social page. You must be active online for social media to work for your business. This is truly where the social part comes into play. What I mean by active is engage online with people's blogs, stories, newsfeeds, tweets and other individual posts. For instance, if you're interested in biking or hiking and you visit hiking blogs and you're visible in the community, you may attract some new followers to your social pages because other people have noticed you. That doesn't mean you should spam and post your business website everywhere, because that will cause the exact opposite effect. Don't post your website on somebody's cycling blog, for instance, and say, "Hey, if you like cycling, you're gonna love this, here's my website." What I'm saying is be active, get involved in forums and communities that you're genuinely interested in. Don't spam post. Make a relationship first, build a connection, and then you become a "social networker" to other people naturally.

You can also find other people who are in other network marketing companies on social media. But as a part of protocol and industry etiquette, don't find people who are selling other products, and try to sell them your product. Nothing makes me angrier than when somebody sees I'm in network marketing, and they send me a message that says, "Oh, you're in network marketing? You have to check out my company!" That's not the way you do it. When someone sends me a message like that, I generally respond, "You don't even know me. What makes you think you could ever recruit me?" On the other hand, if someone I know and trust is involved with something they believe in, I'll listen.

Just like we discussed earlier, you have to be friends first, and recruit later. If you're going out and meeting other people from other companies, you should form relationships first, and later on down the road if you keep a good relationship with

Use social media to your advantage!

them, and if something happens to their company or their products or they get disgruntled, you may have somebody who reaches out to you because you treated them with respect and class and you didn't force your opportunity on them. If you have integrity in what you're doing, you're going to open up a lot of doors for yourself later on. It makes sense to do it the right way. As you are surfing the Internet, be aware that **you have opportunities** all around you to network and build your social footprint.

Social media is one of the most powerful forms of communication our world has ever seen. It brings with it a vast array of opportunities for Network Marketing. Why not use it to your advantage? Once you allow social media to be the catalyst that propels your business to the highest level, you will start getting paid to "Social Network!"

10

Who Is in Your "Starting Five"?

A ssociations between competitive team sports and the direct sales industry have relevant parallels that magnify the importance of team building in business. And because the correlations between the two are so fitting, and so valuable, there has been a glut of sports analogies and slogans within our industry. And why not? The competitive spirit, the importance of team chemistry, the value of being coachable and the crucial impact leaders can have on people around them are all qualities you see in the best teams in sports *and* business.

Having played basketball for much of my childhood, I am drawn to the lessons of the game, which ring true to me at a deeper level even today because of what they taught me growing up. In fact, over the last several years, I have had the pleasure of passing along these lessons by coaching youth basketball teams, participating in programs that engage and develop the hearts and minds of young boys and girls. My role as a mentor has provided me with the opportunity to give back to local communities that have blessed me with so much throughout the years. In the process of volunteering my time and energy, I found that being a coach on the court bears a striking similarity to being one in business. In direct sales, one of the most valuable lessons that has proved fruitful for me has been a concept that I have focused on and implemented throughout my career, and I call this lesson **"Who is in your "starting five"?**

Gleaned from the idea that in a basketball game you must choose the best makeup of team *chemistry,* using five players to start any game for you, your "starting five" are players who comprise the right balance of skills that complement each other. Some people think that it means your best five people, which is sometimes true; but it also means the right make and mixture of role players who perform well together, thereby giving you the best chance of winning the game. In addition to your "starting five", you have other players on your bench who are not in the game currently, but who will play crucial roles throughout each game for your team to win. Basketball teams, whether they're professional, collegiate or otherwise, do not play the same five players the entire game. Coaches choose players based on game-time situations that can change frequently. Some decisions are in response to something that happens in the game or are reactions to the players the other team's coach decides to put in the game. At other times, decisions are pre-emptive and are based on choosing players for anticipated situations. The coach makes these decisions based on the talent and abilities of each member of the team, all the while understanding the overall complexity of situations that happen throughout the game itself. Coaches, who are able to analyze situations and their players effectively, win consistently no matter what players are on their team. In other words, those coaches can win with any team of players because they are able to get the most productivity from that team depending on the situation.

Now, let's take a moment and look at your organization in the same light and examine how these concepts that parallel basketball can also impact your business. When it comes to integrating members who work well together, creating roles for people with specific strengths, putting positive pressure on people who can handle it, allowing more experienced players a chance to play, and working with new team members to inspire and mentor them, ask yourself: How can these concepts leverage my team's chemistry and talents for the benefit of everyone involved?

It will create a synergy that will produce greater results as a unit...

From your first days in this industry, I encourage you to build your team "roster." Your roster should consist of your entire team, and it should have your "starting five" and your other players can be grouped based on "geography" or "strengths" so you can create more of an impact by running your team with purpose rather than just letting things happen. Pause for a moment and write your "roster" down now. Even if you have hundreds of people on your team, this will be something that will enhance your ability to work with purpose. Don't worry about putting your roster in order right now because later in this chapter we'll talk about ways to analyze everyone's skill sets. Just engage in this exercise and you'll begin to build a network of possibilities that will, in turn, help you build the framework of your business.

Regardless of whether you have a few people on your team or 100,000 people, you should be able to compile your roster of key players just like a coach does a team. I keep my roster in my office on my dry erase board and on my computer so I have it with me when I travel or when I am at home working virtually with my teams across the world. This is how I develop strategies, schedules, reminders, contests, events, trainings, calls, and every plan we've discussed in this book. The most important players on my roster are my "starting five". You may have a "starting five" for every market where you have customers or distributors. I construct my entire organization geographically in these types of teams so it is easier to manage and easier for me to keep on track with precision and focus.

Your "starting five" will have strengths *and* weaknesses and their specific roles will contribute to each other and some will overlap just like a basketball team with players assigned to different positions based on their talents. Look at basketball legends LeBron James and Shaquille O'Neal, for instance. They have completely different styles and abilities. LeBron James is a versatile player who sometimes plays point guard calling plays, bringing the ball down the court and setting up the offense. On the other hand, Shaquille O'Neal was one of the most physically imposing players to ever play the game, which meant he was responsible for protecting the basket from the opposing team, for getting rebounds around the basket and giving his teammates a large target close to the basket that they could get the ball to for easier shots. Likewise, your "starting five" will be comprised of dissimilar personalities, motivations and talents that come together to form an integrated unit that, if used properly, will create a synergy that will produce greater results as a unit than if they were all working individually.

Your "starting five" can be similarly applied with the varied customers or team members you work with each day. They all serve different purposes, and they all have something they contribute to your organization. A good coach is able to get more from the group as a whole than the players would provide on their own. In other words, if you can use everyone's strengths in the right ways for the entire team, you create a better chance of winning big in your industry. That means you need to figure out what the ideal makeup of your organization is going to look like. Assign everyone a role and ensure you balance their assignments and team goals to keep people from feeling overwhelmed or under appreciated. As their coach or team leader, determine areas that are legitimate strengths of your team members, as well as their weaknesses. This will help you manage your organization, and also allow you to outline what you need to work on with specific individuals so you can improve their weaknesses and enhance their strengths. This entails everything from organization, speaking, training, presenting, systems, creating culture, and recruiting.

Here are some simple examples of ways to maximize your team's performance and help them impact your entire organization:

1. **Speaking/Presenting:** If someone in my organization has a good stage presence, I will ensure they're in front of larger groups of people as much as possible. And during presentations or events, I often pair them up with members of my team who are not as polished or who are

uncomfortable on stage, in order to build leadership in the experienced speaker and improve the confidence of the inexperienced speaker. This allows the more accomplished speaker to carry the event, but it also gives the more inexperienced participant a chance to hone their skills.

2. **Training:** Some members of your team may be great at breaking down building techniques, making them simple and easy for anyone to understand, especially new people. In my opinion, this is one of the most important aspects of training and teaching. Some successful individuals have an unorthodox style that makes it difficult for new people to duplicate. You need to know this before you allow someone to train or teach at events. The style of someone who shows rapid growth or success is *not* necessarily the best to share with the rest of your team. Another way for these individuals to participate in training would be to share their story and success as a testimonial of your product or service.

   Allow people to train who are effective communicators and people who your new team members will respect and follow. If you allow people who have not "earned' the opportunity to be on the stage to train in a public place in front of your organization, it could backfire and de-motivate people who actually deserve to be there. When you put together trainings and events, make sure you consider the dynamics of your entire team. I try to edify and promote leaders to training positions based on achievement, but make sure it is someone you can trust and will set a good example for the rest of your organization. Remember anyone you edify and put on stage will also be a reflection of you and your company.

3. **Closing:** Good closers are priceless. They have the ability to navigate prospects to make informed decisions about joining your company, and help prospects see the value of being a customer. This is a skill you need to use as

effectively as possible at events, presentations and even trainings. There are ample opportunities for you to allow closers to close from the front of the room, while letting them model their skill in front of other team members who may be weak in this area. Most of the time, closing is about confidence. Allowing your closer to model their skill allows their confidence to rub off on the team, which can spread through your entire organization. Find people who have big closing percentages and make sure you find ways to get new members around them so it will boost their confidence and show them what they should be doing with their prospects and customers.

If you don't have someone on your team who is strong in this area, find someone in your company who is getting strong results and find a way for members of your team to be around them to hear their stories. In the past, when one of my teams was struggling, I figured out a way to have them attend another group's event that was having massive growth and success. Once they saw their event and the people who were signing up, it gave them a whole new perspective and a whole new level of confidence. Suddenly my group in the market that was struggling began having massive success as well because they had newfound belief in the products and opportunity. You have to be able to build on the strengths and improve weaknesses to improve every area of your business.

4. **Systems/Organization:** Figuring out who you can depend on for setting up events and running systems inside your organization is not as easy as it seems. Not everyone will be good at this, so it's important to identify who has this talent as soon as possible. Some of my top performers, for instance, aren't very good at organizing events. When leaders struggle with orchestrating events, meetings and trainings, by extension it leads to poor attendance at most

of these events. Much of the time, you can personally put systems in place to alleviate this problem.

When members of my team have struggled in this area, I have had them observe me organize an event. This has been as simple as just having them listen in on a three-way call of me negotiating with meeting locations, or allowing them to listen to me walk through a list of action items for the event and the corresponding deadlines for those items. Ensure you are aware of dates, deadlines and any time-sensitive information that is crucial for the success of events and trainings in your organization. If you can stay on top of this area and find people in your organization who might not be the top sales performer but who are very dependable, you may be able to create a system where the sales leader, who might not be the most organized person, can work with the "organizer" to hit deadlines and creative massive events in their respective markets.

5. **Recruiting/Prospecting:** Everyone's talents are different. Case in point: recruiting and prospecting. Some people are just naturally better recruiters, as shown in our earlier discussion of "influencers." If you're just getting started, finding someone who is good at recruiting and prospecting may be as simple as figuring out who has the biggest warm market that you can get in front of to share your products or services. Also, ask yourself: "Who has enough credibility to get people to listen to what I have to say?" You'll want to identify these team members as soon as they sign up because their warm markets can be exactly what you need to jump start your business. These types of people may or may not have the most experience inside your team, but they can make a very quick impact on your entire organization. Sometimes the best recruiters and prospectors need some direction and encouragement to really take the information to their contacts. You may have a gold mine sitting untapped in someone with a massive

warm market that doesn't really know where to begin. Get this type of person around you and other successful recruiters and let them see how others do it so it will give them the confidence they need to become the great recruiter they should be.

It's up to you to align your objectives with members of your team who can best accomplish them. Whatever you have to do to get your team operating effectively as a unit, do it! Analyze those areas and stick to your plan.

Once your organization grows in size, your "starting five" may change, and at that point you should also determine who on your team will receive the benefit of your time and how much of it they get. When your organization grows into the thousands, it is *crucial* that you have mastered this skill, because at that size it is impossible to communicate with everyone personally. So you have to determine the best "starting five" on your team that can help spread the impact you have as a leader deeper into your organization. This may mean having a "starting five" in each and every market you work in, or having two "starting five" teams that can act as separate but mutually beneficial arms of the organization so you are able to successfully implement all of the strategies we will cover in this book.

> *You can't wait for success to happen. You have to manage your team.*

My "starting five" is the primary focus of my organization and they get the majority of my attention and time because that's what it takes for me to create results. For this reason, I consistently evaluate this group for their strengths, weaknesses and growth. What's more, I am always on the lookout for members whose performance is beginning to plateau or lag. As a result, I have had to re-position my team, bring new leaders into my "starting five" and move others off the list, countless times throughout my career. I consider this organizational method for my eyes only, and by no means do I discuss the hierarchy with the team, and most of the time people who are in *my* "starting five" do not even know they are in my "starting five".

Luckily, the difference between what we do and an actual basketball team is that in a basketball game only five people can play at a time. In our business, everyone can play simultaneously, but knowing who can come through in the clutch is just as important to know as it is for a basketball coach. I am also using "five" as a hypothetical number. The number of people you regularly communicate with personally may actually be 20, 50 or even more. Remind your leaders to stay on the lookout for the people who deserve more of your time and those who deserve less of your time. One thing we're all guilty of is spending too much time with the wrong people and not enough time with the right people. Because I see myself as a talent scout and a coach, I make it my responsibility to evaluate talent for my business. Of course you can never be sure of the skills that you see in a person, or who will live up to your expectations, but **to compete you must be able to build your business with a team of available, talented players**, just like a coach must select at least five players to play at a time in order to win the game.

Bench Players

I never tire of looking for ways to add new players to the team by personally recruiting them to be part of the business. I also consider new recruits added from other members of my team who I might be able to mentor and groom to become a member of the "starting five". These are what a basketball coach would call his "bench players." They're incredibly important to the team, playing a vital role in unique situations when the "starting five" have to take a break from the game. Their roles are just as important as the "starting five" and it's important to have them prepared so that when they enter the game the team won't miss a beat and every bench player *must* be ready to play when it's their turn. This means you must always be on the lookout for your future "starting five" because you never know when you may be forced to count on one of your "bench players" because something has happened to one of the other players you were counting on. In our industry this could mean just about anything happened to someone you saw as a "starting five", but for some reason or another they are no longer capable of fulfilling that role for your team. If you put all of your eggs in one basket, and spend all of your time and energy working with one person or a specific group, you put the rest of your organization at risk by not grooming your other team members to be ready to step up when it is their turn to take the starting role. So, you have to plan accordingly. Touch base with your up-and-comers a few times a week, rather than every day like you would your "starting five", and try to meet them in person once a month, at minimum. I try to communicate with my "starting five" in some way almost every day. The larger your organization is, the harder this is to accomplish, but if you master the art of being mobile, you can be a pro at communication and effective group management.

Making the List

What if your current "starting five" are not your ideal "starting five"? What if they don't meet your expectations? This is one of the reasons why it's important to look at yourself as the coach of your organization. Perform this exercise, it will help: Take your "starting five" and across from that list write what you envision those five starters should look like. In other words, if you could create your ideal team, what would it look like? Consider the following:

- What types of leaders would you have?
- What would their strengths be?
- How would you integrate their strengths and improve their weaknesses?
- Who would be their alternate player in a clutch situation?
- How many sales or customers would each of them be responsible for adding weekly or monthly in their respective organizations?

- What levels of responsibility would each of them have?

- How would they interact and help lead the rest of the team?

Some of these people may already be what you envision, some may be new and have potential to be your next superstar and some may have talents you are not using currently. You may even be thinking about someone who is already in your organization who's not performing, so you wouldn't put them in your "starting five" right now, but you see them as a person who could be there in the future. Part of compiling your "starting five" is visualizing where you're going, and understanding the strengths and weaknesses of your organization. This is how you take your business to the next level. Understand and study your business. If you fail to see what's going on, and you're operating on blind faith, you're reduced to hoping that people are holding meetings and attending events, hoping that they are active and, ultimately, hoping that they have decided to stay with the organization and not quit. If this is you, you're really not doing anything. You're not running the organization, you're not coaching the team, you're not facilitating anything, you're just waiting for success to come to you. If you're waiting, then your business is not moving forward, and you're not building on the energy and strengths of your current organization. Make it a point to understand how your team works together. It will benefit your business today and in the future.

Managing Your "Starting Five"

Here's another sports analogy. You've acquired some excellent players who have outstanding talent and skills, but they're just not performing. You can't count on them, they're not dependable, they don't do what they say they're going to do, they don't respond or communicate or answer calls. As a coach, you can't have that type of activity and miscommunication within your organization. You have to make a decision, not based on promise or potential, but based on what's really happening. Sometimes your best performing players may face challenges and it's clear they're in a rut because their productivity has waned or reached a plateau. As a coach, if you're not getting results or nothing new is happening, you have to change it up. You may have to stop trying to *make* someone become something that apparently they are not ready to become. You have to be willing to do what it takes to make your team successful. It may sound harsh, but it's a reality. Sometimes you've got to force activity around you to create change. It may be uncomfortable, but it will take you in the direction where you want to go.

> *Make it a point to understand how your team works together.*

There are lessons I teach my "starting five" that I don't share with the rest of my team. As a result, I've had members become so successful that they've graduated out of my "starting five". Once they graduate, they make their own "starting five", and identify their own "bench players," and I begin with a new "starting five". I should point out that most of the top earners and performers in my organization were not "starting five" players when they came into the business. Believe it or not, **productivity and success are not based on luck**. So, don't waste your time waiting for your "next superstar" to show up and miraculously appear on your team. This industry is unlike anything your team members and distributors have ever done before, so don't expect them to be experts.

Achieving success takes guidance with purpose, and deliberate instruction by a leader or mentor. Everyone I know in this industry who has had massive success refers to someone or some group who has mentored them and made it possible for them to achieve the level of success they have attained. Some of the hardest workers and top performers in my organization were struggling personally and financially when I met them. But now, after they've proven themselves through hard work and have risen through the ranks in my depth chart, I trust in their ability completely. I'll go to battle with them any day, and if I were beginning any business or venture, they would be my first choices. So don't just sit around waiting for your business to take off, waiting for a "superstar" to show up and propel your business. You are the next superstar of your company, and you are the coach of "future superstars."

Take control of your organization today and you'll reap the rewards you and your organization deserve.

****

I hope you have enjoyed the journey we have shared in this book. I wanted to put this book together to share experiences I have learned along the way to hopefully save you some of the trials and tribulations I experienced when I was new in this industry. This information is meant to act as a guide to help you create the business and lifestyle you truly deserve. The only difference between me and most of you reading this book is that I have just been doing this longer than you have. Apply the principles and ideas we have discussed and you will cut years from the learning curve of this industry. I will be sharing new content and information on my website at www.WesMelcher.com so register for my newsletter and stay in touch to receive all of my current training content. I may not be with each of you on your journey personally, but I hope that you will take a piece of me with you as you conquer your fears and impact the lives of future generations through this incredible industry!